**A Reader-Friendly Guide to
Identifying, Understanding, and Treating
Adult Attention Deficit Disorder**

Adult ADD

Thomas A. Whiteman, PhD
Michele Novotni, PhD

WITH RANDY PETERSEN

P.O. Box 35007, Colorado Springs, Colorado 80935

OUR GUARANTEE TO YOU

We believe so strongly in the message of our books that we are making this quality guarantee to you. If for any reason you are disappointed with the content of this book, return the title page to us with your name and address and we will refund to you the list price of the book. To help us serve you better, please briefly describe why you were disappointed. Mail your refund request to: PiñonPress, P.O. Box 35002, Colorado Springs, CO 80935.

© 1995 by Thomas Whiteman and Michele Novotni
All rights reserved. With the exception of pages 245-249 as specified on pages 245 and 248, no part of this publication may be reproduced in any form without written permission from Piñon Press, P.O. Box 35007, Colorado Springs, CO 80935.
Library of Congress Catalog Card Number: 95-12685
ISBN 08910-99069

Cover design: David Carlson
Cover illustration: Dolores Fairman

Whiteman, Tom.
    Adult A.D.D. : a reader friendly guide for identifying, understanding, and treating adult attention deficit disorder / Thomas Whiteman and Michele Novotni, with Randy Petersen.
    p. cm.
    ISBN 0-89109-906-9
    1. Attention-deficit disorder in adults—Popular
works. I. Novotni, Michele. II. Petersen, Randy. III. Title.
RC394.A85W48   1995
616'.85'89—dc20

95-12685
CIP

Printed in the United States of America

3 4 5 6 7 8 9 10 11/04 03 02 01 00 99

CONTENTS

ACKNOWLEDGMENTS

We would like to acknowledge the following colleagues for their help with this project.

James Schaller, M.D.—He has provided medical management and consultation for many of our ADD clients and also provided insights into the chapter on medication.

Mary Stewart-Van Leeuwen, Ph.D.—Professor at Eastern College who reviewed the final draft of the book.

Bill Morgan—He is a therapist and evaluator at Life Counseling Services. He provided much of the material for the chapter on behavior modification and shared his insights and stories.

Sharon Mathias—She gathered data, tracked down leads, and helped us coordinate the many meetings necessary for a project like this.

Kathy Houlihan—Graduate assistant at Eastern College who researched many of the articles on ADD.

To each of these people we extend a heartfelt thank-you, knowing that their work was well above the call of duty!

READ THIS FIRST!
AN INTRODUCTION

There are silent struggles that go unnoticed by the general public. These battles are waged in the lives of people who have ADD—Attention Deficit Disorder (also known as ADHD). They are among the most misunderstood people in the world.

Sometimes they're considered dumb, because they forget things or their concentration lapses—but they're not dumb.

Sometimes they're considered rude, because they blurt out inappropriate statements at inopportune times—but they're not trying to offend anyone.

Sometimes people get frustrated with them, because they seem to have so much potential but they never seem to live up to it. But no one is more frustrated than ADDers themselves.

We have talked with hundreds of people with ADD. It has touched our own families, our own lives. We share in the struggle. We hope this book will promote understanding, inspiration, and practical help to many who suffer from ADD and to the many who care about them.

Reader-Friendly Format

We've learned that people with ADD often start books but don't finish them. This book is primarily for the person who has ADD (or thinks he or she has it). So, our first goal is to make it highly readable for those who are easily distracted.

But don't let that fool you. If you're looking for scholarly research and serious treatment, as they say in the soup commercial, *It's in there!*

Adult ADD has been recognized by professionals fairly recently. As we'll discuss later, the experts still aren't sure exactly what to call it or what different forms it takes, especially in adults. Still, between us, we authors have counseled hundreds of people with ADD and have studied the issue thoroughly. We will tell you what the experts say and what they suspect. And we'll give you the stories of real people with ADD.

The format of this book may take some getting used to. To make it more reader-friendly, we're italicizing all stories and illustrations. If you get bogged down in stories and want "just the facts," skip the story sections. If you love stories and need examples to keep you interested, zoom ahead to those if the text gets dry.

We also provide summaries at the end of each chapter. It's common for ADDers to sometimes read a page or two and then forget what they just read. The summaries will give you quick takes on the material as you go.

Confronting the Controversy

There's controversy about ADD swirling through the therapeutic world. Sometimes it seems to be the "Disorder of the Month," with *everybody* claiming to have ADD and using it as an excuse for poor work and bad manners. We'll discuss this tendency in our first section, "Living with ADD."

In our *second* section, "Getting the Right Diagnosis," we will examine proper diagnostic methods. Who is qualified to diagnose and treat ADD? Are there any recognized tests for this disorder?

Just what are the symptoms of ADD? For researchers, ADD is something like that proverbial watermelon seed: As soon as you pin it down, it squirts away. You can be hyperactive or *not* hyperactive. How can so many symptoms be used to describe the same disorder? In our *third* section, "Recognizing the Symptoms," we'll talk about what ADD looks like. You may see your own reflection in that part of the book.

How should ADD be treated? Some try stimulants, others try behavior modification methods or therapy. Do these things work? Should you seek meditation or medication? There are drugs that lessen the effects of ADD, but aren't there some cautions involved? And what is the role of counseling in all this? In our *fourth* section, "Exploring Treatment Options," we'll review the many treatment methods available.

Finally, our *fifth* section, "Overcoming ADD Difficulties," focuses on the problems faced by the person with ADD. With any treatment method, there are still life issues that the ADDer needs to deal with—rocky relationships, challenges on the job, continuing organizational and learning problems. We offer specific strategies for success in each area.

About Us

Both of us, Tom and Michele, are psychologists at Life Counseling Services of Paoli, Pennsylvania.

Michele is also a professor at Eastern College in Saint David's, Pennsylvania. We have conducted seminars on adult ADD in our area with overwhelming response. Michele has made this a specialty, partly because her son and father have ADD. Tom has a mild form of ADD himself. He has considerable experience treating childhood ADD, especially during his eight years as a school psychologist in the Philadelphia School District.

We have seen hundreds of clients learn to manage their ADD using one or another of the methods we describe. There is certainly hope and help for the ADD sufferer!

As you read, you should know that we are using real stories in this book. We have gained permission from a few clients with ADD to tell their stories *and to use their names*. We are grateful to Maria Bassler, and Helen and Laura Thompson. They all felt strongly that there was no reason to be ashamed of ADD, and so they agreed to be interviewed for this book, letting us use their names and their stories.

In many other cases, however, to protect the privacy of the people mentioned, we have changed names or minor details, but the stories are true.

If you have ADD, think you might have it, or know someone who might have it, you've come to the right place. Read this book in your way, at your own pace. But please read it. You should find a few things here that will make your life better.

PART ONE

LIVING WITH ADD

CHAPTER ONE

NAMING THE BEAST

A MAN COMES HOME from work, picks up the mail, turns on the evening news, and starts opening his mail as he half-listens to the TV. Then he remembers that he had to call his office to leave a message for the office manager. He drops the mail between the cushions of the sofa and heads for the phone in the kitchen.

When he gets to the kitchen he sees the refrigerator and feels hungry. He pokes around the fridge and makes a snack. With the food, he heads back to the family room to watch TV, completely forgetting about his phone call.

Later that night he asks his wife if she has seen the mail. "I haven't seen it," she says, and he becomes angry at her.

When she conducts a search and finds the mail in the cushions of the sofa, he sheepishly apologizes. "I guess I just forgot about it. Sorry."

• ◆ •

Does this scenario sound familiar? Scenes like this haunt the lives of people with Attention Deficit Disorder (ADD). Long considered merely a childhood problem, ADD is now being recognized in a growing number of adults—sometimes with devastating results.

The mail-in-the-sofa story seems harmless enough. But what about that call the man forgot to make? What if it was crucial for a major business deal? The man might find himself without a job.

What if the mail contained an important document and was lost for days instead of hours? What if the flare-up at his wife was the ninth one that week and the marriage was already in trouble?

It's no joke. People with ADD often find themselves unemployed or underemployed because they cannot consistently focus on their responsibilities. Their finances may be in shambles. Their relationships are frequently rocky.

Maybe you already know the story.

HOW MANY OF THESE STATEMENTS SOUND LIKE YOU?

"I set things down and forget where I put them."

"I start projects but have difficulty following through."

"I find myself jumping from thing to thing."

"I have difficulty concentrating."

"My life is fairly disorganized."

"I've had difficulty working up to my potential."

"Sometimes I say or do things without thinking."

"I feel misunderstood by others."

A World of Hurt

For Michael* (all names followed by an asterisk
have been changed), forgetfulness and a lack
of organization have been hallmarks of his life.
Though he is really quite intelligent, he always
had difficulty in school. He found ways of scrap-
ing through high school and he even tried going
to college, but he struggled with most of his
classes.

Michael managed to work in various jobs
while he finished up his college degree at night.
Now he works as a salesman and spends a lot of
time on the road in dialogue with his clients. He
is able to make a decent living doing this, and it
is by far the best job he has ever had. It is also
the longest he has ever worked at the same job—
eight years.

The recurrent problem in his job is his disorganized style and forgetfulness. Frequently
he is late for appointments, but with a car phone
he can overcome most of the fallout from this
trait. He is almost always late with his paperwork and mileage reimbursements because he
is so undisciplined.

At first Michael's boss and his secretary had
fits with his habits, but now they overlook his
faults because he makes up for it in sales. He is
very good with people—outgoing and friendly.
His clients like having him stop by and are
happy to give him orders. (If only he could get
them in promptly, he wouldn't have to make
excuses about how "the office messed up their
order.")

Michael's marriage has been a similar series
of frustrations, except his wife is much less for-
giving. After all, she has to live with him! "He's

15

always jumping from thing to thing, and never completes anything!" Peggy exclaims in frustration.

They have been married now for eighteen years and have two children. When the children were young, things were at their worst. Peggy almost left Michael because of his lack of help around the house. At one point she felt she couldn't even trust him to watch the kids while she went out. Oh, Michael would intend to be a good baby-sitter, but then he'd pop a video in the VCR and go off to read Field and Stream *magazine and eventually forget all about the kids.*

Finally Michael and Peggy reached a truce as Peggy gave up trying to change him. She began to expect less and less from him, but she wondered what happened to that charming, intelligent young man she thought she had married.

This is an uneasy peace, however, as there are weekly, sometimes daily, flare-ups. Peggy has very little patience for his forgetfulness or excuses. She interprets his behavior as being deliberately resistant. Michael is also frustrated with his inability to please her. He wants to, but he just can't.

•◆•

ADD is often misunderstood. Children with ADD are often considered dumb when they are really quite smart. They can gain a reputation as difficult children because they don't remember a teacher's instructions, can't concentrate on the subject matter, or can't sit still.

The same misunderstandings can carry into

adulthood. ADDers can seem rude or ignorant, lazy or rowdy. Often it's assumed that a person with ADD is hiding some deep rebellion, and his lateness or lack of discipline is a passive-aggressive way of taking revenge.

But people with ADD are as frustrated with their problems as those around them.

Gifts and Limitations

Amy* is a very successful businesswoman. She owns her own marketing and advertising agency and has eighteen employees. I (Tom) went to her office for consultation on marketing a new service we wanted to provide to the community. As I sat in the waiting room, glancing through a magazine and listening to the soothing music, I almost nodded off.

Then the whirlwind hit.

A woman dressed in blue jeans and a pullover sweatshirt whooshed into the lobby and all of the staff snapped to attention. She handed out orders—"Type this. Take care of that for me. Have this mailed out right away." The staff moved quickly to do her bidding.

Then she barked, "And where's my eleven o'clock appointment?" That's when I snapped to attention.

Somehow I knew this dynamo had to be Amy. "I guess that would be me," I said, standing up and shaking her hand. As we headed to her office, she pelted me with questions. Before I could finish an answer, she was asking the next question.

Once we were in her office, I saw how Amy lived. There was a computer covered with papers. A bulletin board with loads of memos attached. She had a radio on an all-news station providing background noise the whole time we talked. But the most annoying part of the conversation was the way she would ask me a question and then look over my head as I spoke.

This was so annoying that I actually turned around and looked behind me. There was a TV set on with the sound turned down. Amy mentioned that she watches the financial news and keeps an eye on the ticker all day long.

After she had asked about my project, I began to interview her. Sensing her hyperactivity, I began to ask about her work style, her relationships, and her personal life. She had always excelled in creative areas, she told me, but lagged behind in academic subjects. College was a mixed bag, since she avoided any math or science, leaning more toward literature, cultural, and artistic subjects. While she was able to handle these subjects, they really didn't lead to jobs after college.

She took jobs wherever she could get them but was very frustrated in each one. She described herself as being way ahead of most of her bosses—something they never seemed to appreciate.

Finally, Amy found a boss who really appreciated her style. He would literally give her the ball and let her run with it. She found people around her who could make up for her weaknesses—mostly following through with her ideas and initiatives. She was usually three steps ahead of everyone else, moving in several different directions at one time.

Amy's big break came when one of her biggest clients offered to help her go out on her

own. She started her own agency and now
enjoys running her own show. She said she was
destined to be on her own, since there weren't
many bosses who could handle her work style.
"I need at least three people running around
behind me, following through on all my ideas,"
Amy proclaimed. "I know I tend to drive people
crazy. but I have good ideas, and I'm most
productive when I'm freed up to do what I do
best—dream and create."

Amy's personal life is not nearly as successful as her professional life. While she is in her
mid-thirties, she has not had a serious relationship since college. She blames this on men.
"Men are intimidated by my success. Why do
men have such fragile egos?" she asked me.

"I'm sure you intimidate a lot of men," I
replied, "but I bet that's not true for all men."
I then encouraged Amy to look at her own
distractibility and the fact that she is pulled in
so many directions. "How can you carry on a
serious relationship if you can't direct time and
energy into making one thing work well and
follow through on what you commit to doing?"

That's when Amy opened up. She admitted
that she's fine on the first few dates. She has
lots of fun because she has so many diverse
interests—museums, theater, golf, tennis, hiking.
She's good at many things. Men love that.

But when it comes to following through on
her commitments, or when the relationship
requires a focused conversation or working
together on shared goals and objectives—well,
Amy finds that much more difficult.

"That's why I have an office staff," she

explained. *"They handle the details for me. It works in business, but it's murder in a relationship."*

•◆•

Hyperactivity is often, but not always, associated with ADD. People with ADD often feel a need to be doing five things at once. They tend to work best with a radio going and perhaps a TV on. And, with the right support system, such people can be very productive.

ADDers can also be extremely creative and very outgoing. Their high energy tends to be attractive (but sometimes tiring). Often they'll have many friends but few deep relationships. Amy's story is not unusual in that respect. High energy can get you through the first few dates, but when it's time to hold a real conversation, things get tough.

Faking It

Aaron's* life has been a series of failures. It all started in school with constant efforts to get passing grades while feeling stupid and out of touch. While others were learning and progressing in school, Aaron felt frustrated and humiliated by his inability to pick up even the most basic skills.

Early in life, Aaron learned how to fake it. He nodded agreement when he wasn't sure what the teacher was talking about. He pretended to know how to read when he wasn't sure of the words. He actually made it through high school by faking, avoiding, and—when he had to—cheating. He graduated with only an elementary level in reading and math, even though others considered him to be of average ability.

After high school, Aaron got a job in a gas station. His parents urged him to go to college, but he put them off by saying that the gas station job was just temporary, a way of saving money for school. But in truth, Aaron did not believe he had the ability for college. He felt like a fake and was more comfortable in a setting where there were few challenges.

At work Aaron was gaining more and more responsibilities. He had a good way with people but didn't understand many basic concepts. He would use his learned coping skill—faking it—whenever he had to do a cash deposit or read anything of substance. The owner, however, was impressed with his work and began to trust him more and more. Aaron was still filled with self-doubts and personal insecurities. He became night manager, which gave him two new responsibilities. He had to keep track of a lot of cash, and he was sent out to do towing jobs several times a week. Both turned out to be big problems.

Aaron had difficulty adding the cash and filling out the deposit slips. He was afraid he would show everybody just how incapable he was. So he began to drink heavily—a six-pack of beer each night. It was Aaron's way of self-medicating his low self-image and personal pain.

He assumed no one would notice if he began pocketing cash from the station. It was an easy way to pay for the beer.

So Aaron would hang around the station drinking and then get a call for towing. Fortunately his drunk driving didn't result in any accidents. But finally he got caught driving under the influence of alcohol. Aaron lost his *driver's license and then lost his job.*

The court ordered him to see an addictions counselor who treated him for alcoholism. In gathering Aaron's history, he also questioned his educational and learning problems. The counselor realized these lay behind his low self-image, self-doubts, and feelings of inadequacy. Drinking was Aaron's way of numbing the pain of feeling stupid. He considered himself a disappointment to his parents, his friends, and to himself. A six-pack would help him forget all that for a few hours.

As it turned out, Aaron was referred for further evaluation and was diagnosed with ADD. He was able to receive treatment, but that's not an automatic happy ending. There was a lot of damage to undo. He had to get honest about the things he had never learned when he was faking it in school. Now Aaron is taking some remedial classes at night school. He and his parents are hoping he can eventually take college courses or technical training in order to get a better job.

•◆•

The Common Thread

At first glance, Michael, Amy, and Aaron seem like totally different people with totally different problems. One is a forgetful, disorganized, middle-level management man; another is a highly successful, hyperactive woman; a third is a young man who has experienced a series of failures, including a drinking problem. Yet each of them has been diagnosed with adult Attention Deficit Disorder.

HOW CAN ONE DISORDER APPLY
TO SO MANY SITUATIONS?

Perhaps Michael is merely forgetful or sloppy. There are lots of people like that in the world, right? Maybe Amy just drinks too much coffee. And how many people like Aaron could we find— slow learners with drinking problems? It seems too easy to call all of this ADD.

Isn't this just another of those self-help gimmicks, the disorder of the month, a subject for the next TV movie? Are we merely giving Michael an excuse he can tell his wife? Aren't we just giving Amy a reason to feel she has overcome something? Maybe this diagnosis gives Aaron some hope, but is there any substance to it?

Many observers, including a number of professional therapists, have been understandably skeptical about the diagnosis and treatment of ADD. We know that some counselors jump on bandwagons. We also know that many clients find relief in being branded with an official "disorder." (Suddenly they have an explanation for their behavior. They are no longer lazy, stupid, sloppy, or rebellious. They have a medically recognized reason for their shortcomings.)

But when you meet Michael, Amy, Aaron, or a hundred other ADD sufferers, this theoretical issue suddenly becomes real. These are people who don't always fit in. Their minds work in a different way. In some cases, their lives are falling apart because they cannot focus consistently as "normal" people do. It is not just lack of discipline. It is not just sloppiness. It is not just a free spirit. There is a problem that holds these people back. It's as real as a broken arm.

Attention Deficit Disorder has been recognized in children for almost a hundred years. It was often associated with hyperactivity. It was thought that a child would outgrow ADD. Children with hyperactive ADD seemed to enter adulthood without it. But then people started finding adults with ADD symptoms—lots of them.

The scientific research on the subject of adult ADD is fairly new. Yet there does seem to be a physical aspect to the disorder—an imbalance that affects the brain's neurotransmitters (more on this research later). And there are drugs that can make up for this imbalance. So ADD is not just "all in your head"—well, it is in your head, but not just in your imagination.

Short of testing the chemicals in your brain, how can you tell if you have ADD? That's where it gets confusing. Here is a partial listing of symptom complaints of ADD sufferers.

- Forgetfulness
- Difficulty focusing on any one task
- Difficulty following conversations, particularly when there are several people involved
- Tendency to take on too many projects and then not finish most of them
- Time-management problems
- Easily frustrated
- Frequent moves or job changes
- Pattern of underachievement or underemployment
- Difficulties with relationships
- Tendency toward substance abuse
- Low self-image or insecurity at approaching new tasks

- Impulsive decision-making style
- Tendency to take risks
- Not sticking with long-term projects
- Tendency not to read or finish books
  (magazine or newspaper articles preferred)
- Not understanding social nuances
- Difficulty with paperwork (getting things
  in on time)
- Difficulty managing finances and checkbook

Another area is especially significant: People with ADD often lack insight into how others perceive them. In other words, you may think you're fine, but you might be driving other people crazy in some of these areas. So, before you rule out any of these symptoms, check the list with someone close to you.

Is This for Real?

Probably everyone in the world can relate to at least some of the characteristics ADD sufferers have described. And remember that this is a partial listing. One recent article reviewed the literature and found a total of sixty-nine symptoms and thirty-eight causes cited.[1]

So how do we discern who has ADD and who doesn't? Professionals continue to debate that issue. There are various screening tests available (and we'll present you with a preliminary screening test in this book), but these tests differ in their breadth.

Some experts consider ADD quite rare, afflicting less than 2 percent of the public. Others say that one in five people may have ADD. We suspect there is a large group of people with "mild ADD," exhibiting some of the symptoms but experiencing only minor difficulty in their lives.

We also worry that the ADD diagnosis will become so broad that it loses all meaning. Without specific diagnosis and legitimate intervention, we could all find ourselves filling out questionnaires in popular magazines, only to find out we all have ADD in one way or another. As one quipster put it, "ADD must stand for 'Any Dysfunction or Difficulty.'"

If this happens, the ADD diagnosis will lose its meaning and the treatment will become compromised. Yet ADD is a real problem, affecting real sufferers. For their sakes, let's all be careful how we use the term.

ADD appears to be a many-headed beast. It takes many forms, but there seem to be common threads of causes and symptoms. Once we accurately name a problem, we can know better how to deal with it.

There's a curious reaction among those we have diagnosed with ADD. Yes, as you would expect, some of them worry about what's wrong with their brains. But for many it's an "Aha!" moment. There is relief and even joy as they realize their lifelong problems do not stem from laziness, stupidity, or selfishness but from a brain disorder. It's ADD.

And once we name the beast, we can tame it.

JUST THE FACTS

- ADD takes different forms—disorganization, impulsivity, creative hyperactivity, or general underachievement, to name a few.

- While some may try to diagnose ADD at "the flick of a Bic," we should all be careful about overdiagnosing and underdiagnosing this problem.

- Though it may be a "fashionable" problem to have these days, that does not negate the fact that some people genuinely suffer from ADD and face great difficulties.

NOTE
1. Gay Goodman and Mary Jo Poillion, "ADD: Acronym for Any Dysfunction or Difficulty," *Journal of Special Education* 26 (1992), pp. 37-56.

CHAPTER TWO

BEYOND THE BLAME GAME

O.J. WAS A VICTIM. Or so we've been told.

The Menendez brothers were victims, and so they shot their parents to death in their living room.

The Bobbitts were both victims, and—well, you know what happened there.

Even Michael Fay, the young man who was caned for vandalizing cars in Singapore, claims he's a victim—of Attention Deficit Disorder.

At the risk of seeming hardhearted, we feel that this whole victimization craze has gone too far. We say this because we *do* care about those who are *genuine* victims. But when everyone claims to be a victim, it actually dilutes our compassion. If everyone is a victim, then no one is.

This issue greatly affects how we deal with ADD. There is no question: ADD is a legitimate disorder. Society needs to understand it and make reasonable allowances for it. But should ADD sufferers be excused for crimes they've committed? We don't think so. Should ADD sufferers be allowed to stay home on permanent disability pay because they "can't" work? No, that's a slap in the face of every ADDer who has struggled and succeeded in the workplace.

We tend to agree with Roger Connor of the American Alliance for Rights and Responsibilities who said on an ABC News Special, "Everybody has rights. Nobody has responsibilities. And our society ain't gonna work. This whole victimization — it's like a disease that's weakening America's moral fiber. Living consists of encountering the weaknesses, the failings that we all have as individual human beings, and the problems that inevitably enter our lives, and dealing with them. That's the stuff of life."[1]

ADD is a problem, but it's not a death sentence. ADDers should not sit at home and vegetate. They should try to manage their condition and get out there and make a difference in the world. They can make it if they try.

Most of the ADDers we have met have been hard workers, not shirkers. They are not looking for excuses; they are looking for a fair chance to succeed. There are reasonable accommodations that can and should be made by employers, schools, and families of those with ADD. Unfortunately, there are a few ADDers who are seeking *unreasonable* accommodations and making things more difficult for the many who are struggling honestly to overcome their ADD.

Integrity in Action
Diane* had a problem. Her ADD symptoms were affecting her work and she was on the verge of being fired. Her greatest difficulty was in prioritizing her tasks; she tended to major on the minors.

Through counseling, she determined to make

a last-ditch effort to communicate with her boss about her problems. She did not make demands but suggested certain ways the boss could help her be a better worker. (Her counselor helped her devise these ideas.)

First, she asked if she could meet with the boss for a few minutes at the start of each day to go over her list of things to do. The boss would identify the most important projects for her to tackle. Diane also asked for "time spacing" on her monthly reports — intermediate deadlines in mid-month. Previously, she had waited until the last minute to prepare these, but now she asked her boss to hold her accountable to those earlier deadlines.

Diane also asked for a flex-time arrangement. She knew she had to be there for most of the working day, but she got her best work done when no one else was around. The boss agreed to let her come to work an hour-and-a-half late and stay an hour-and-a-half late, so she could have that prime time at the end of her working day. In fact, the boss agreed to all her suggestions. He had to spend a few extra minutes with her, but he got a much more effective employee out of this arrangement.

• ◆ •

Too many companies have a business-as-usual approach. They are inflexible to the special needs of certain employees, such as those with ADD. But increasingly, businesses are realizing that ADDers (and others) have a lot to offer, and a few minor adjustments could pay off in the long run. Diane's boss realized this, and it resulted in a win-win situation.

But Diane's attitude was important, too. She was not blaming anyone or demanding anything. She was offering her best efforts and suggesting some new arrangements. Unfortunately, some others are taking very different approaches. Let's look at three *unreasonable* ways of looking at ADD. Too often ADD is used

- As an excuse for irresponsible behavior
- To claim a handicap
- As a defense for wrongdoing

The Excuse

When Frank* was first diagnosed as ADD, he became very emotional. He felt as if twenty-some years of pain were being released at one time.

In school he had thought he was stupid, since he had a lot of difficulty keeping up with the classes. Then he thought he was unemployable as he moved from job to job. Then, through a period of unemployment, he fought feelings of laziness. Finally, he got a sales job that he seemed to do well with, but he had a very difficult time getting along with his boss.

Frank also had trouble in his marriage. His wife labeled him "passive-aggressive." Whenever he was late, forgetful, or insensitive, she assumed he knew exactly what he was doing and did spiteful things just to upset her.

Then Frank heard a radio show about ADD. He made an appointment with the doctor who had been on the radio and was diagnosed. He had ADD.

Years of failure and frustration were all explained away in one brief evaluation! Now he had a reason for the way he acted!

This would be a wonderful success story if it weren't for the fact that now Frank had more than an explanation — he had an excuse.

He told his boss he couldn't be expected to sit through staff meetings. He claimed that he couldn't do any of his paperwork, and whenever his sales figures dropped, he blamed it on ADD.

His marriage went from bad to worse. All those times his wife accused him of being passive-aggressive — well, now he knew he was falsely accused. And she still didn't fully understand how "handicapped" he really was. He now had an excuse for being habitually late, for not following conversations, for being insensitive, and for not being able to follow through on household tasks or chores. His wife would give him lists, which he would usually ignore. After all, he was ADD and couldn't be expected to remember such lists.

•◆•

Some people who have ADD have used the diagnosis as an excuse for irresponsible behavior. They use it at home, on the job, anywhere they might have responsibilities they'd like to avoid. They use ADD as a license to be self-centered. They make no effort to change.

We're treading a fine line here. ADD may explain a person's irresponsible behavior but it doesn't excuse it. It is very difficult to live with ADD. Those who grow up with this disorder face years of low self-image, frustration, and impaired achievement. They tend to be chronic under-achievers, yet most of them find ways to cope with it. They learn to excel in certain areas. Having ADD might be a legitimate explanation for why a person struggles at certain tasks, but it is not an excuse to stop trying to manage the symptoms or to accept less than one's best.

One man, an executive in a publishing company, bemoaned the day an employee was diagnosed with ADD. "He had been a fairly good worker," the boss reported. "He didn't really excel at his job, except for the fact that everyone liked him. He was a real people person. And he was steady. He wasn't very fast at any of the clerical skills necessary for his job, but he plugged away."

One day the employee announced that he had been diagnosed with ADD. The boss was skeptical at first, because he had never suspected that the employee had any kind of disability. He had always seemed "normal" to him.

The employee explained, however, that he couldn't do more than one thing at a time, and that he needed a private office with a door, and that he couldn't handle the phones if they interrupted his concentration. "I tried to accommodate him," the boss said, "thinking it would be worth it if it helped him to work faster. But the opposite happened. He did less and complained more."

Soon the demands grew. The employee couldn't have any talking outside his office. Then no one was to interrupt him when the door was shut. The whole company tried to play by his rules, but still his productivity decreased steadily.

"He always had excuses for why he couldn't get any of his projects done," the boss said. "Finally, I had to ask myself, 'What am I paying him for? I have an employee here who needs a

*private office with no interruptions and no phone
calls, and he still can't get his work done. I don't
even afford myself those kinds of luxuries, and
I'm the boss!' I had to let him go."*

•◆•

What was causing the problem here? ADD? Not
really. The employee had suffered with ADD all his
life, but he was doing an acceptable job before his
diagnosis. What changed? His attitude. Once he
knew he had ADD, he began to use it as an excuse.
He began to focus on his rights as a victim of this
disorder, not on his responsibilities as an employee
of this company.

We don't mean to minimize the difficulty this
man was facing. But it seems as if he stopped trying as hard once he was diagnosed with ADD.
Having ADD is not an excuse to avoid work. The
diagnosis should instead motivate those with ADD
to learn all they can to overcome its effects.

The Handicap

A young man in our area is suing his school district because they failed to educate him. He had
been diagnosed with ADD while in junior high and
had subsequently dropped out of school. According to the suit, his condition had caused him to not
complete assignments, to skip classes, and to wander the halls. This had resulted in frequent sus-
pensions. The young man now wants the school
district to pay for his attendance at an expensive
special school.

This case raises interesting questions. Whose
responsibility is involved here? Certainly some
schools fail to accommodate students with special
needs. Such students can fall through the cracks

35

in a school that provides instruction for hundreds, even thousands, of children. Perhaps the school did fail to meet its responsibility to care for the unique educational needs of this individual.

But doesn't the young man have some responsibility, too? And doesn't his family have a responsibility to find the treatment he needs to function properly in his society? As we will see in this book, various forms of treatment are available to help those with ADD. In most cases, the symptoms of ADD can be overcome. Couldn't the young man and his family have found some way to lessen the misbehavior that sabotaged his education?

At our counseling center we occasionally see individuals who come for ADD evaluations and then, once they are diagnosed, ask us to fill out "disability" papers for them so they can make some kind of claim at work or from the state. In severe cases, we have no problem doing so while we work with the person. But, curiously, most of those who come to us with disability forms have only mild cases of ADD—cases that are not very disruptive to begin with and usually can be easily treated.

We are seeing a national proliferation of claims surrounding ADD, which will probably continue as a result of the Americans with Disabilities Act of 1990. Congress passed this legislation to protect Americans with disabilities. The Act makes it illegal to discriminate against the disabled, requiring employers to make reasonable accommodation for the disabled. A great idea and an important law. Unfortunately, the language is so ambiguous that it invites abuse of the system. What qualifies as a disability? What is a "reasonable accommodation"?

In the ABC News special "The Blame Game:

Are We a Country of Victims?" John Stossel interviewed Mark Simidion, a blind man. Simidion has
a job taking flight reservations over the phone for
Northwest Airlines. Each day he takes a train,
walks two blocks, and catches a bus to get to work.

In his job-hunting days, some prospective
employers asked him, "How would you get to
work?" He would politely say that was none of their
business.

"That's the way I am," Simidion explained. "I
don't want to make excuses for myself. I don't want
to put up walls or barriers that are going to get in
my way."

This is the sort of person the Americans with
Disabilities Act (ADA) was created for. It's not clear
that it was responsible for getting Simidion his job.
"Still," as reporter John Stossel comments, "it may
have helped. Who knows if Northwest Airlines
would have spent the extra $4,000 to install this
equipment [a Braille computer screen] and give
him special training? The investment paid off,
though. In just two months, Mark has become one
of the office's top ticket sellers."

In the same report, Stossel talked with several
employees of a county in New York State. They're
claiming to be afflicted with an ailment called Multiple Chemical Sensitivity, and were staying home
(claiming disability) until the county removes all
the chemicals from its office building. The county
had attempted to meet the demands of the employees, replacing a ventilation system and changing
its photocopying processes, but the "disabled"
employees weren't satisfied and sued the county
(under the ADA) for $800 million.[2]

In the first two years of the ADA, 33,000
claims were filed. Most of these, no doubt, were

legitimate claims by hard workers like Mark Simi-dion, people merely requesting a fair shake in the workplace. But how many of the claims were bogus or petty?

And where does Attention Deficit Disorder fit in? Some are claiming this as a disability and demanding major changes in their places of employment.

We feel that employers should show some flexibility and sensitivity in dealing with the ADD sufferer. Usually, modifications would be rather modest: noise reduction, help with organizing tasks, or perhaps varied assignments in order to hold one's interest.

We must point out that ADDers are often extremely creative people, and in some cases very outgoing. Just as a company might seek a balance on its staff of introverts and extroverts, of thinkers and feelers, so a company might seek to support its ADDers with other employees who are very structured and down-to-earth. As these people learn to work together, it could be a great boon to a company.

But people with ADD must not make their companies revolve around them. Merely in terms of their own therapy, it is dangerous to "play victim" all the time. If you force others to accommodate your disorder all the time, you are giving up that spark of motivation that will help you find wholeness. Yes, you do have certain rights in the workplace, and you may discuss these in reasonable terms with your employer. But you also have responsibilities. If you are being paid for a job, you have the responsibility to earn that pay. And there is no reason you cannot do that. It is the responsibility of the person with ADD to seek treatment—

through medication, behavioral techniques, or some other method—and to cope effectively with its symptoms.

The Defense

There's also a legal trend that causes even ADD advocates to cringe. Increasingly, ADD is used as a defense in criminal cases. The most notorious example occurred when Michael Fay was arrested in Singapore and sentenced to be caned. His lawyer claimed that his diagnosis of ADD should be considered in a plea for leniency by the court. You might think this to be a rarity, but at the time of this writing there are reportedly more than fifty-five similar cases in which ADD is being used as part of the defense.[3]

Could there be some truth to these claims? In fact, students who have been diagnosed with ADD have a higher incidence of aggression, substance abuse, and criminal behavior.[4] But there is no evidence that their biological disorder is the cause of the problem. Rather, most believe that students with ADD are merely more frustrated than their peers. They struggle to understand social nuances, and that tends to put them at odds with the people around them. They have a more difficult time in school, and thus they may be labeled as "problem" kids. In addition, ADDers are generally more active and impulsive. These factors combine to create children who are much more at risk for defiant and criminal behaviors.

Although most of the criminal cases are attributed to teens and young adults, the same factors affect the lives of many older ADD adults. For example, our experiences in counseling, lead us to the impression that adults with ADD have a greater

39

incidence of substance abuse. We attribute most of this to the years of frustration, misunderstanding, and even depression.

ADD does not *directly* cause crime or abuse, but it may indirectly affect it. It's a multi-step process. ADD creates difficulty from the very start. The child with ADD is immediately at a disadvantage. This is not an insurmountable disadvantage, but it is considerable. Those ADD-based difficulties can initiate a chain reaction of other problems, which may lead eventually to crime. By adulthood, many have learned coping skills, but that basic disadvantage continues, and the chain reaction often continues.

For these reasons, we promote understanding and reasonable allowances for the victims of ADD. But we are leery of the "ADD defense" in a legal setting. Even a victim of ADD is responsible to uphold the law. ADD is a factor in the same sense as a variety of other childhood disadvantages. The child who is abused by his or her parents faces issues of self-esteem, boundaries, and social appropriateness. The child who grows up in a home where the parents routinely break the law will have difficulty learning the standards of the larger society. The child who grows up with parents who are enslaved to alcohol or drugs will have an equally hard time. Any of these may wind up as criminals. Society must listen to their stories, understand their disadvantages, and do what it can to help. But society must also hold them accountable for their crimes.

In the courts, ADD is a reason for some leniency, perhaps. It is certainly a reason to consider creative punishment and to recommend treatment. But is ADD an excuse for crime? No.

Your Responsibility

If you have ADD, you have a responsibility to "manage" it. That means controlling your behavior. In mild cases of ADD, you may be able to manage it through counseling, behavior management, and sheer determination (with help from a spouse and/or friends). In severe and moderate cases, you probably need medication and counseling.

How do you know if it's severe? The next chapters will discuss screening and diagnosis, but for now let's just say this: If you are messing up at your job because of ADD, if your marriage or family relationships are on the rocks because of ADD, and certainly if you are committing crimes because of ADD, you have a major problem. You need to take responsibility for your condition. This is something you can't afford to put off.

In every weakness there is strength. This is true of ADD as well. For all of the negatives, there are also positive aspects to the disorder. Find your positives and capitalize on them. Are you creative, fun to be with, friendly, exciting, smart? Then put yourself in positions where those qualities can come out. As much as you can, avoid situations that require the abilities you don't have. Try not to take on tasks you know you won't complete. Try to avoid overwhelming projects or extremely distracting environments. This is all part of managing your ADD. Know your strengths and weaknesses, and lead with your assets.

Vicki*, a woman with ADD, came to me (Tom) for a career assessment. She was frustrated with her job and was looking for a new direction. As we examined her strengths, we found creativity,

*people skills, and an ability to communicate and
persuade others. She particularly liked to be
outside. She liked to have a variety of tasks. She
enjoyed moving about.*

*Yet Vicki found herself in a job where she sat
at a desk all day, rarely moved from her chair,
and had very little contact with other people.
She had no outlet for her creativity, she was just
expected to follow the routine. No wonder she
was looking for a change!*

*I recommended a job as a salesperson, one
where she would be on the road, making decisions, on the move, meeting with people. As it
turned out, Vicki got work selling medical supplies
to physicians' offices. She is well-liked, does
quite well, and loves her job. All her clients look
forward to her visits.*

•◆•

Vicki is not playing the blame game because there
is nothing to blame on anyone. I suppose she could
have demanded that her previous employer make
major changes to accommodate her. If she was
then fired, she could have hired a lawyer to sue for
damages under the Americans with Disabilities
Act. She could have used her ADD as an excuse.
Instead she used it as a springboard.

JUST THE FACTS

- It has become fashionable to be a "victim," but ADDers should resist that temptation.

- Some use ADD as an excuse for inconsiderate behavior, causing difficulty in their relationships.

- Some claim ADD as a handicap and seek disability pay or outrageous accommodations from employers.

- Some are invoking ADD as a legal defense, claiming they were not responsible for their illegal acts.

- We feel these attitudes are inappropriate. While society should be sensitive to the special needs of ADDers, the ADDers bear responsibility for their own actions.

- ADDers have a responsibility to "manage" their ADD and to seek treatment.

- Thousands of ADDers struggle day by day to succeed in a difficult world, not seeking excuses. We applaud them.

NOTES
1. Quoted from interview with John Stossel, "The Blame Game: Are We a Country of Victims?" ABC News Show #ABC-55, 1994.
2. Stossel.
3. Russell Barkley, "Attention Deficit Disorder," *TIME* magazine, 18 July 1994, page 45; Barkley, "The ADHD Newsletter" (New York: Guilford Publications).
4. Michael D'Antonio, "The Trouble with Boys," *Los Angeles Times Magazine*, 4 December 1994, pp. 16-22.

PART TWO

GETTING THE RIGHT DIAGNOSIS

CHAPTER THREE

Is It ADD—
Or Isn't It?

ADULT ADD WAS AN almost unknown syndrome ten years ago. As a school psychologist, I (Tom) was trained to think that attention deficits and hyperactivity only existed in children, and the effects wore off or "matured" sometime in adolescence. I taught this "truth" to others and gave this hope to many parents.

Yet I noticed something unusual about many of the parents I was telling this to. They seemed different. Not necessarily hyper, but different in a similar way to their kids. Sometimes it was the mom, but more often it was the dad who seemed to have problems following my report or suggestions. Some were distracted, jumping impulsively from subject to subject. Others would relate to my explanation of their children's symptoms by saying, "I understand; I was the exact same way when I was in school." They complained of continuing problems with reading, spelling, and (most commonly) organizing their lives. *The apple doesn't fall far from the tree*, I reasoned. I did not know of any official research to back me up, but it wouldn't have surprised me to find that the parents had an adult version of ADD.

My casual observations were borne out in research literature that spread into the national spotlight in the mid-1980s. Apparently other people had noticed ADD symptoms in adults. Some researchers were suggesting that there was such a thing as adult ADD, that children did not always outgrow it. For some time it was a matter of debate among mental health professionals. But now there is a growing body of research indicating that adult ADD not only exists, it is treatable.[1]

With the diagnosis and treatment of this "new" disorder, many have found relief from lifelong symptoms that have deeply affected their careers, their relationships, their lives.

I became even more aware of the issue when I left the school setting and entered a private practice to counsel adults. Many clients with histories of learning problems were having extreme difficulties with their relationships and on their jobs. Could this be adult ADD? But how could so many be afflicted with a disorder that was unknown a decade earlier?

Then a local newspaper was preparing a story on adult ADD and the reporter called my co-author (Michele) for some quotes. Her name appeared in the story and within days our counseling center had more than 150 phone calls from people asking to be evaluated for this syndrome. We knew we had hit a sensitive nerve.

A few of the callers were obviously just overreacting to the media hype. But most of them had valid concerns. They had at least some of the symptoms of ADD and wanted to know if this could be the reason they had so many problems in their marriage or on the job.

For many, the answer was yes. But not everyone who is distracted at work or finds it hard to follow conversations or struggles with remembering certain kinds of information has ADD. Sometimes it's just a personality quirk or a lack of discipline or a crowded schedule. Sometimes there's another psychological issue involved.

It's easy to jump to conclusions when you read an article about ADD in a newspaper or magazine. You assume that you have ADD since you share some of the symptoms, but that isn't necessarily true. Some of our 150 callers did not turn out to have ADD. Others had different problems that we could help with. Yet for many others, that phone call was the first step in a life-changing process of diagnosing and treating a disorder that had plagued them for years.

Jason* first came to our counseling center after hearing from a friend that we diagnosed and treated adult ADD. He had been diagnosed as manic-depressive several years earlier and had since been taking medication. Then he started hearing and reading about ADD.

As he read stories of other distraught and even depressed people who were misdiagnosed by other psychologists, Jason latched onto the idea that this was his case. When he brought this up with his own doctor, the doctor barely acknowledged Jason's concerns. Now he was in my (Tom's) office, convinced that his real problem was ADD—not depression. He wanted me to help him stop his medication for depression and start him on his new treatment plan for ADD.

• ◆ •

This is a common problem and one of the reasons adult ADD is so controversial. There are four assumptions I might make about Jason's situation.

1. Not all mental health professionals are aware of the existence of adult ADD, and therefore may misdiagnose the symptoms. Perhaps Jason's doctor never considered ADD as a possibility.

2. Some professionals are very aware of the literature on adult ADD but do not believe in the authenticity of the syndrome. One psychiatrist told me, "We all have problems with attention and organization. We merely fall along a continuum on these skills. To diagnose and medicate these characteristics is like medically treating someone for selfishness. We're all selfish. It's just that some are more selfish than others."

3. The diagnosis of ADD is very complex. The symptoms can be similar to other emotional conditions (such as depression). Therefore, while many would want to self-diagnose this disorder, they really need to be tested by a psychologist or a psychiatrist who has knowledge and experience with adult ADD. Perhaps Jason *was* depressed, as his doctor had indicated, and he was merely being swayed by the media to claim this trendy new disorder. It would certainly sound better to Jason to be suffering from ADD than to have a serious emotional problem.

4. ADD is often associated with other disorders, such as depression, anxiety, passive aggressiveness, and addictions. Sometimes it is hard to determine which is the *primary* condition or the one that should be treated first.

Jason could very well have ADD. And maybe the problems associated with ADD have caused him to feel hopeless and depressed. But if his depression has reached a point where it is a more serious issue, his doctor may choose to treat the depression first and foremost and then address the ADD at a later time. Other doctors may disagree and treat the ADD first, or treat them both at the same time, but it is a judgment call that each professional has to make on a regular basis.

Unfortunately, diagnosing ADD is not an exact science. While ADD has specific symptoms, these same symptoms occur in a variety of other emotional problems and disorders. So, when examining a possible ADD case, the therapist must not only look for the symptoms of ADD, but also *rule out* several other possible causes of those symptoms. That's why it's inappropriate to say, "I have ADD," after merely checking through a list of symptoms in some book (even this book!). It takes a careful study by a qualified professional.

Mixed Reviews

Unfortunately, even if you go to a qualified professional, there's no guarantee he or she will agree with the qualified professional next door. Mental health practitioners are split on the issue of the diagnosis and treatment of ADD. Most would acknowledge that ADD exists, but how often? The variance is ridiculous. Estimates range between 2 and 22 percent of the U.S. population.

One indisputable fact is that the diagnosis of ADD is on the rise. As the airwaves and the printed press present the issue, people are lining up at clinics to be diagnosed and treated. Doctors have reported a doubling in their ADD caseload, and reports indicate that the nation's use of Ritalin (the leading anti-ADD drug) has increased dramatically.

Is this good or bad science?

Let's put it this way. People suffered from ADD twenty years ago and fifty years ago and even back in 1776. (Some have suggested that William Shakespeare, Isaac Newton, Ben Franklin, and Albert Einstein all had ADD. But we don't know how anyone could be certain of this.) What did they do about it back then before they had books like this one?

They lived with it. Some of them (like Shakespeare and company) may have *thrived* with it. Others probably found it impossible to get any work done. Maybe some of them went to doctors, and maybe some of them were even treated, but not for ADD. Depending on the time period, they'd be treated for depression or dementia or humors or evil spirits. And those treatments wouldn't work, because the real problem—ADD—was unknown.

In that historical light, maybe the discovery of ADD is a great scientific breakthrough, finally naming this pesky beast that has thwarted human achievement for centuries! The recognition and effective treatment of ADD can set children and adults free to live fruitful lives.

Or maybe we're making all this up.

Maybe the ADD craze is bad science, not good science, because doctors are jumping to diagnose something they don't understand.

Psychologist G. Reed Lyon, Ph.D., a director at the National Institute of Child Health and Human Development, said he is alarmed by both the increased frequency of the diagnosis and the fluctuation of the prevalence of the diagnosis within geographic areas. (This would indicate that ADD follows local trends—like an article appearing in a local newspaper—rather than a natural pattern of occurrence.) Lyon believes the disorder is often mistaken for other problems with similar symptoms, such as anxiety, emotional concerns, depression, even a hyperactive thyroid.[2]

But other researchers are saying that we've only scratched the surface. Robert Resnick, president of the American Psychological Association, says most clients are being diagnosed properly. While recent publicity may have led to some knee-jerk reactions, he says, the hype has more likely resulted in a heightened awareness among educators and mental health workers, so that more people are being properly identified and treated.

Yet Resnick cautions: "What concerns me is when a fifteen-minute interview in a doctor's office leads to an attention deficit diagnosis." In Resnick's office, clinicians spend about six hours screening a client for ADD.[3]

The authors of the book *You Mean I'm Not Lazy, Stupid or Crazy?* echo that concern: "We can't emphasize enough that a diagnosis is not a *do it yourself* enterprise. A person with schizophrenia, for example, might have attention deficits but her treatment would be radically different from that of an ADDer. Using stimulant medication in her treatment would likely have the effect of dramatically worsening her condition. The point is, accurate diagnosis is an essential component of treatment."[4]

We want to add our voices to these cautions. ADD is a complex syndrome with very different symptoms and various degrees of severity. It is not something you should diagnose or treat on your own.

If you have a different condition, such as anxiety or depression, the treatment would be very different. In fact, all emotional disorders affect your activity level, the way you think, and the way you process information. The diagnosis must determine that the symptoms you have are attributable to ADD and not to any other condition. This is referred to as "differential diagnosis," and it's the main reason you need to consult with a trained professional.

When I (Tom) was working with the Philadelphia School District, I would frequently get referrals for learning problems and/or atten-tional difficulties. One teacher had a student she thought was severely disabled.

"He can't seem to sit still or pay attention," she exclaimed. "And to make things worse, things he once knew he now doesn't seem to know how to do. What kind of disorder would cause a child to forget how to write his name once he had already mastered the task?" she asked.

As it turned out, it was no disorder. The boy was "merely" experiencing the separation and divorce of his parents. It was a particularly ugly situation that affected the boy's emotions, behavior, and thinking.

No, he did not have ADD—and that's the point. I could have tried to treat him for any number of complex mental disorders, but I would have been wrong. He was going through an extremely painful time in his life, and he was being emotionally wounded. I would only have injured him more if I had tried to fix some mental disability that didn't exist.

•◆•

Sometimes It's Not ADD

You may have a number of the symptoms of Attention Deficit Disorder, but that may just be the way you are. In their less exaggerated forms, ADD symptoms are merely part of normal human functioning. As one doctor said to me, "We all have some degree of disorganization, inattentiveness, or impulsiveness. Don't be too quick to assume you have a disorder."

Another reason ADD can be difficult to diagnose is that the symptoms are so diverse and may even seem contradictory. There are some symptoms that all ADDers display, such as inattention, but even this is inconsistent. A person with ADD can focus on something for a while, and very intently, but an hour later be flitting from one thing to another.

Other symptoms vary widely from patient to patient. Some have hyperactivity and impulse control problems; others can't remember things or always lose things; many others find it hard to follow through on projects or to organize tasks.

For example, one person might need total quiet in order to study or get work done while another needs background music to work effectively. One person might start several different projects and never finish any of them. Another person may jump immediately from point A on an idea to Z, the final product, without considering the intermediate steps.

HELEN'S STORY

Helen was the first adult I diagnosed with ADD. I (Michele) had been counseling her daughter, Laura, for depression and had discovered that

Laura had ADD. During the clinical interviews with Helen, as I described her daughter's condition, Helen kept saying, "That sounds just like me." Helen viewed films and read books about her daughter's disorder. She soon began to believe this was her own disorder as well.

Laura's story is inspiring. Once she was treated for ADD (with medication and counseling), her grades improved dramatically, her social life improved, and her depression lifted substantially. The change in her schoolwork was so dramatic that school officials called to tell Helen that they were concerned about her daughter—she had to be cheating! There was no other explanation, they felt, for the fact that Laura had gone from C's and D's to A's and B's.

Helen began to look at her own life and the difficulties she had always struggled with. Recently divorced, she was hesitantly considering a return to school. This was a fearsome prospect because, like her daughter, she had never done well in school, even though she seemed quite bright. Like Laura, she was accused of not working up to her potential. But now Helen was intrigued by her daughter's success. "Could this also be me?" she wondered.

After I evaluated Helen, it became clear that she was indeed suffering from the same symptoms as her daughter and had been for her entire life. She had frequently been treated for depression due to her poor self-esteem and underachievement. But those treatments had missed the real problem—ADD.

I was able to diagnose Helen's ADD, but I could not prescribe medication. Unfortunately, her daughter's doctor was a pediatrician, and not able to treat an adult like Helen. Eventually, Helen found a psychiatrist who said he would be willing to evaluate and treat an adult with ADD even though he had never done so before.

After the psychiatric evaluation with this doctor, Helen returned to me in tears. The psychiatrist had stated that she did not have ADD, she was merely depressed. So Helen kept trudging along in psychotherapy, taking medication for depression, which hadn't worked before and wasn't working now. In fact, as she watched her daughter's life dramatically improve, Helen became more depressed and frustrated about her own life.

Almost a year later, we found another psychiatrist in our area who was willing to treat adult ADD. This psychiatrist was more familiar with the symptoms of adult ADD and the medical management of the disorder. I called Helen and asked if she'd be interested in trying again.

At first she didn't want to do it. She'd had her fill of psychiatrists. She didn't want her hopes raised and dashed again. But the image of her daughter's turnaround was strong in her mind. Maybe Helen could try once again to see if she too had ADD.

After this psychiatric assessment, the second doctor agreed that she did have ADD, and he prescribed medication. Almost immediately, Helen began to notice improvements in her ability to focus and concentrate.

Within a short period of time, Helen was no longer depressed, although she still struggled with emotional issues. She did well in her return to school, making the honor roll for the very first time.

57

In fact, she was even able to take up a unique extracurricular activity. Helen had become an activist in ADD education. Wherever she goes, she talks about ADD, urging people to seek proper diagnosis and treatment. She wants to help others avoid the plight both she and her daughter had faced due to unidentified ADD and an uninformed physician.

• ◆ •

JUST THE FACTS

• Adult ADD is a new and popular diagnosis, perhaps too popular.

• The diagnosis of ADD is not an exact science, and mental health professionals differ in their assessments and opinions.

• The symptoms of ADD are diverse and complex and can reflect other disorders.

• Beware of self-diagnosis and jumping to conclusions. ADD can be accurately diagnosed only by a well-trained professional.

• When ADD is properly diagnosed and managed, the results in the life of the one who suffers can be extraordinary.

NOTES
1. David Woods, M.D., "The Diagnosis and Treatment of ADD-Residual Type," *Psychiatric Annals,* vol. 16:1 (January 1986), pp. 23-28.
2. Randell Edwards, "Is Hyperactivity Label Applied Too Frequently?" *APA Monitor* (January 1995), pp. 45-46.
3. Edwards, pp. 45-46.
4. Kate Kelly and Peggy Ramundo, *You Mean I'm Not Lazy, Stupid or Crazy?* (Cincinnati: Tyrell and Jerem Press, 1993), pp. 3-4.

CHAPTER FOUR

THIS IS YOUR BRAIN ON ADD

SIMPLY PUT, ADD IS a condition of the brain in which the person has disturbances in areas of attention, information processing, and impulse control. Problems with impulse control are most often referred to as hyperactivity. For some, the hyperactivity is "internal" only, meaning their brains are active even if their bodies are not, though the problem may seem more obvious in those who display behavioral hyperactivity.

Children's hyperactivity often seems to disappear as a child matures, leading some to assume that childhood ADD is outgrown. But new research indicates that the symptoms don't disappear; they just *evolve* with age. Some ADD children do outgrow their learning difficulties or learn new coping skills, or they eventually just slow down; but it is now believed that many carry some symptoms (or similar symptoms) throughout their adult life.[1]

Twenty percent to 65 percent of children with ADD continue to show signs of the condition into adulthood.[2]

A History of the Disorder

In the mid-seventies, terms like *hyperkinesis* and *Minimal Brain Damage* (MBD) were used to describe children with learning disabilities and attentional problems. These children were usually hyperactive, conduct disordered, and typically displayed severe behavioral and emotional problems.

A kinder, gentler era changed the Minimal Brain Damage to Minimal Brain *Dysfunction*, but that quickly evolved into the more general term *learning disabled*. This category included all kinds of children's problems. Subcategories of learning disability included math and reading disabilities, developmental delays, auditory and visual processing problems, and of course, attention deficits, some with and some without hyperactivity.

Most of the work and research surrounding ADD was done with children, but in the late seventies, adult ADD started to be recognized. This was referred to as Residual ADD, but today is more simply referred to as adult ADD (or ADHD).

Professionals diagnose ADD following the guidelines of the *Diagnostic and Statistical Manual of Mental Disorders*, Fourth Edition (DSM IV), which is the bible of diagnosis for psychologists and psychiatrists.[3] The DSM IV renamed ADD as ADHD (Attention Deficit/Hyperactivity Disorder), but we will continue to use the popular term "ADD" for easier reading. The DSM IV describes three primary symptoms of ADD: inattention, impulsivity, and hyperactivity.

In order to have ADD, a subject needs to exhibit at least six of the symptoms listed for inattention *or* at least six of the symptoms from the combined list for hyperactivity-impulsivity.

Symptoms of Inattention

a. often ignores details; makes careless mistakes
b. often has trouble sustaining attention in work or play
c. often does not seem to listen when directly addressed
d. often does not follow through on instructions; fails to finish things
e. often has difficulty organizing tasks and activities
f. often avoids activities that require sustained mental effort
g. often loses things he needs
h. often gets distracted by extraneous noise
i. is often forgetful in daily activities

Symptoms of Hyperactivity-Impulsivity

Hyperactivity
a. often fidgets or squirms
b. often has to get up from seat
c. often runs or climbs when he shouldn't (for adults, feelings of physical restlessness)
d. often has difficulty with quiet leisure activities
e. often "on the go"; acts as if "driven by a motor"
f. often talks excessively

Impulsivity
g. often blurts out answers before questions have been completed
h. often has difficulty waiting his turn
i. often interrupts or intrudes on others

In addition to "six from column A or six from column B," the subject must:

- have shown some symptoms before age seven;

- have difficulty from these symptoms in two or more settings (such as, work and home)
- show "clinically significant impairment" at work or school or with other people
- not suffer from another mental disorder that could explain the symptoms.

Those last two criteria (and especially the last one) prevent self-diagnosis. You can go through the lists yourself and consider your own history and present situation. But only a professional can judge whether your impairment is "clinically significant." And only a trained mental health professional can screen for a variety of other disorders that could be causing your symptoms.

Once a psychiatrist or psychologist has screened a subject according to these criteria, he or she might diagnose:

ADHD, Predominantly Inattentive Type;
ADHD, Predominantly Hyperactive-Impulsive
    Type; or
ADHD, Combined Type.

Causes of ADD

There have been many theorized causes of ADD including

- prenatal birth trauma
- environmental toxins
- food additives, caffeine, and sugar
- an inherited personality style
- parenting style or the home environment
- the information, TV, "sound bite" explosion of our society

While these issues may be contributing factors for ADD in an individual, most research now concludes that ADD is an inherited biological condition in which the cortex of the brain does not function normally. Contrary to what logic would dictate, the brain of the ADD sufferer is actually less active than the normal brain. Using a combination of scanning devices and radioactive tracers, scientists measured blood flow to the frontal lobes of the brain. In the brain of a person with ADD, this blood flow, indicating brain activity, was lower.[4] Interestingly, in cases where the frontal lobes are damaged (e.g., head trauma), the patients often exhibit symptoms similar to ADD symptoms, including distractibility, impulsivity, and sometimes hyperactivity. However in head trauma cases, these symptoms are often much more severe.

While the actual functioning of the brain is much more complex than this brief explanation suggests, researchers are growing more certain about how this all works. They have concluded that there is an insufficient amount of the neurotransmitter dopamine in the brain of the adult with ADD. This is a chemical that carries the electrical impulses between nerve cells. Therefore, they reason that the ADD brain actually needs more stimulation. And that is why stimulants such as Ritalin have been the treatment of choice for years.

When you think about it, it seems strange. Why give a stimulant to a person who's already hyperactive? Don't you want to calm him down? Give him a depressant, for goodness' sake!

For years, doctors never really understood why the stimulant worked, but it did work, so they prescribed it. Researchers have now found that these stimulants provide the increased dopamine that increases brain activity and blood flow in the brain. But the question remains: Why does *decreased* brain activity result in hyperactivity and distractibility? Why does the stimulation to the brain *reduce* these behaviors and curb impulsiveness?

The experts still haven't figured this out totally, but it seems that the understimulated brain will be driven to seek outside stimulation. It tunes into the radio playing in the next room, it notices the activity outside the window, or it jumps into a new project without considering the consequences. Medical stimulants merely provide the needed internal activity to bring the brain into a more normal mode of functioning.

Imagine a classroom of young children (or teenagers, for that matter). Let's say the teacher has a low-energy day. What do the kids do? They're bouncing off the walls! There is no discipline in the classroom, no focus, because the teacher is fighting a cold and feeling blah.

But let's say that teacher takes one of those super-duper cold remedies. The teacher perks up and summons the strength to discipline the class. What happens? Less hyperactivity in the classroom but more productive work.

The brain may work something like that. A person with ADD has a weak "teacher" in the brain, and therefore the brain functions like an unruly classroom. The proper stimulation gets that "teacher" functioning again, which focuses the brain on what needs to be done.

JUST THE FACTS

- ADD has a variety of symptoms, which can be labeled as inattentiveness, hyperactivity, or impulsivity.
- While many causes have been suggested for ADD, it now appears that there is a physical aspect to the disorder: People with ADD have less of the chemical dopamine that transmits messages through the brain. It seems that this reduced brain activity results in a lack of focus, which paradoxically allows the brain and body to "run wild."
- Proper medical stimulation can help bring brain function into balance.

NOTES
1. Lynn Weiss, *Attention Deficit Disorder In Adults* (Dallas: Taylor Publishing Co., 1992), p. 21.
2. G. Weiss and L. Hechtman, *Hyperactive Children Grown Up: ADHD in Children, Adolescents and Adults*, 2d ed. (New York: Guilford Press, 1993).
3. *Diagnostic and Statistical Manual of Mental Disorders: Fourth Edition* (Washington D.C.: American Psychiatric Association, 1994), pp. 78-85.
4. Zametkin, Nordahl, Gross, King, Semple, Rumsey, Hamburger, and Cohen, "Cerebral Glucose Metabolism in Adults with Hyperactivity of Childhood Onset," *The New England Journal of Medicine*, 30 (1990), pp. 1361-1366.

CHAPTER FIVE

WHO CAN DIAGNOSE AND TREAT ADD?

THIS IS NOT A FORMAL test for ADD, but it *is* a helpful screening instrument to identify those who might benefit from a formal ADD assessment. If you score high, we recommend you contact a mental health professional to have a thorough ADD assessment done. Please do not assume you do or do not have ADD based on this screening assessment alone.

THE NOVOTNI ADD SCREENING ASSESSMENT

1. Do you have a lifelong pattern of having difficulty *"working up to your potential"*?

0	1	2	3
Not at all	Just a little	Yes, I think	Definitely

2. Have you had lifelong difficulty with being able to *focus consistently* on your work or other activities?

0	1	2	3
Not at all	Just a little	Yes, I think	Definitely

(continued)

3. Do you have a lifelong history of being easily *distracted* by thoughts, peripheral sights, or sounds?

0	1	2	3
Not at all	Just a little	Yes, I think	Definitely

4. Have your *school grades, your interpersonal relationships, and/or your career* been affected by these difficulties?

0	1	2	3
Not at all	Just a little	Substantially	Greatly

5. Has it been difficult to keep your *self-esteem* intact due to these difficulties?

0	1	2	3
Not at all	Just a little	Yes, often	Very much so

6. Do you feel that you struggle in the areas of *distractibility and inattention* more than most people you know?

0	1	2	3
Not at all	Just a little	More than most	More than anyone I know

7. Do you have a lifelong pattern of having difficulty *thinking first before you act or talk*?

0	1	2	3
Not at all	Just a little	Yes, I think	Definitely

8. Were you *physically active* as a child?

0	1	2	3
Not at all	Just a little	A lot of the time	Most of the time

(continued)

9. Do you frequently feel *overwhelmed or frustrated*?

0	1	2	3
Not at all	Just a little	A lot of the time	Most of the time

10. Do you have any incidents of head trauma, mental disorders, physical or sexual abuse in your past?

0	1
Yes	No

Now total up your points.

TOTAL:

If you scored twelve points or more, it is likely you would benefit from a formal ADD assessment.

If you scored ten or eleven points, there is a chance you have ADD or a related difficulty. You may want to consult a mental health professional and ask about the possibility of ADD.

If you scored fewer than nine points, there is not a significant indication that you have ADD. Still, if you are disturbed by ADD symptoms, don't hesitate to be properly assessed by a professional. Once you've been formally assessed, you may find you do have ADD or perhaps some other difficulty that can be helped.

Who Can Help?

If you're ready to consult a professional for an ADD assessment, how do you sort through the maze of psychiatrists, psychologists, neurologists, and so on? How can you tell who's "qualified" to tell you about ADD?

If you are currently seeing a counselor, that's a good place to start. You may ask for advice or recommendations from this professional, who presumably knows quite a bit about you. But bear in mind a few things:

- Your counselor may not know much about ADD.
- Even if your counselor has treated ADD in children, he or she may not be experienced with *Adult* ADD.
- Your counselor may have a bias for or against the diagnosis of ADD.
- Your counselor may not be trained or experienced in diagnosing or treating ADD.
- Your counselor may not be able to provide the treatment you need if you do have ADD.

You be the judge. Talk with your counselor about his or her expertise and limitations in this field. Don't hesitate to get a second opinion. A good counselor will be forthright about your options, allowing you to choose what's best for you. Since some doctors are unaware of ADD except in a passing fashion and may inadvertently misdiagnose or mismanage your case, talking with someone who has already been evaluated or treated by a professional may save you considerable heartache and expense.

When you're ready to proceed, where do you turn? There are various kinds of professionals in the mental health field. You should be aware of the pluses and minuses of each.

THE PSYCHOLOGIST

A psychologist is skilled in the way the mind works. While he or she probably knows a great deal about the physical functioning of the brain, the focus of the psychologist is not medical but mental. How do you feel? How do you think? What makes you do what you do?

A psychologist *is* able to diagnose adult ADD. With training in differential diagnosis, a psychologist can consider and rule out other disorders that may look similar to ADD.

A psychologist is also able to treat adult ADD through methods such as counseling, behavior management, and supportive problem solving. While there are different theories and therapies, most psychologists have some training and experience in individual and group counseling skills of a concrete nature (i.e., Cognitive Behavioral Therapy, Behavior Management, and Reality Therapy). For those with ADD, this type of approach seems to be more helpful than an in-depth psychoanalytical process.

By the time an adult discovers that he or she has ADD, there are generally a number of psychological issues that need tending, such as self-esteem, interpersonal relationship skills, lifelong habits acquired to compensate for ADD, and grief issues regarding the losses the undiagnosed ADD created. A psychologist is well equipped to help with these issues.

If you desire or have been advised to seek medication management, you'll need a referral to a medical doctor or psychiatrist. Most psychologists routinely make these referrals.

71

THE PSYCHIATRIST

A psychiatrist is a doctor of the mind and brain. He or she would also be able to diagnose ADD and can treat ADD through medication management or counseling (depending on his or her specific training and skills in this area). Most psychiatrists, however, are psychoanalytically based and are not as experienced in the concrete, behavior-oriented, problem-solving, therapeutic process that is often most useful for those with ADD.

A psychiatrist can complete the entire process of evaluation, medical treatment, and sometimes counseling. However, a psychiatrist is generally much more expensive than other health care providers.

When a client needs to work on the residual issues created by ADD, the psychiatrist may need to make a referral to someone more experienced with counseling.

THE FAMILY PHYSICIAN

What about your family doctor? Controversy abounds regarding whether or not the family doctor should become involved in the diagnosis and treatment of adult ADD.

A family doctor is usually an M.D. with general expertise in treating common ailments. Some family doctors have developed an interest and expertise in diagnosing and treating ADD. Just as a family doctor may diagnose and treat someone for depression (which is also in the *DSM IV*), some family doctors are diagnosing and treating ADD in adults. Family doctors are increasingly willing to provide medical management for clients with ADD once the clients have been diagnosed by a mental health professional.

Family doctors are able to diagnose and prescribe medications for disorders within their "area of expertise." It is up to each doctor to decide the parameters of his or her expertise. Some doctors are less stringent than others in determining their parameters. Some may consider it sufficient to attend an ADD workshop for a weekend. Others may think they're qualified after merely a conversation with a peer or after reading a journal article. Still others will insist on reading numerous journal articles, attending several workshops or conferences, and consulting with peers at length before they will consider treating a patient for ADD.

A family doctor with a knowledge of adult ADD has the advantage of knowing you and your medical history well. For most adults, a visit to a family doctor is less intimidating than seeing a psychiatrist. Family physicians may be a good first step for people who suspect a mild form of ADD.

The biggest limitation of using a family physician for an ADD assessment is that he or she is not aware of differential diagnostic issues in any detail. Attentional difficulties resulting from other mental health disorders may be missed by such a practitioner.

In terms of medical management, a family physician may have limited knowledge regarding effective treatment for other psychiatric disorders or ADD. Therefore, the family doctor may need to refer you to someone with more expertise if you are not responding to first-level medical interventions.

If you are to get the specific counseling you need to make progress dealing with various ADD-related life issues, your family physician will need to refer you to a professional counselor.

THE NEUROLOGIST

A neurologist is a physician specializing in problems of the nervous system. Neurologists are expensive and often require an extensive neurological workup—EEG testing, etc.—which does not seem to be necessary in the diagnosis or treatment of most cases of ADD. This neurological workup, however, can be very important if other neurological conditions, such as a seizure disorder, are suspected or present. A neurologist generally has a more limited knowledge of other psychological causes for ADD symptoms and may have difficulty with the differential diagnosis needed for ADD.

A referral will be needed for counseling.

THE MASTER LEVEL COUNSELOR

A Master level counselor is trained in counseling, with a master's degree in psychology or counseling. If such counselors have been trained in ADD, they are generally able to complete the initial screening stages of an ADD assessment. However, the client should be followed up by a psychologist or psychiatrist to make the differential diagnosis.

Just like the psychologist, a trained Master level counselor is able to treat the symptoms of adult ADD through counseling, behavior management, and problem solving. A counselor generally has training and experience in individual and group counseling skills of a concrete nature.

If it is deemed appropriate, you would need a referral for medication management.

74

THE SOCIAL WORKER

A social worker is often employed by an agency to counsel people involved with that agency. To be qualified to counsel professionally, a social worker needs an M.S.W. (Master of Social Welfare) degree. If a social worker has been trained in ADD, he or she would generally be able to complete the initial screening stages of an ADD assessment. However, after meeting with the social worker the client should be followed up by a psychologist or psychiatrist to make the differential diagnosis.

A social worker may be able to treat adult ADD through counseling, but most social workers have psychoanalytic training, which is generally not a helpful approach for adults with ADD.

If deemed appropriate, you would need a referral for medical management.

PROFESSIONAL COMPARISONS

PSYCHOLOGIST

Advantages
- trained in differential diagnosis
- skilled in concrete individual and group counseling and problem solving
- can help with many ADD-related issues

Disadvantages
- need to refer for medication management

Costs
- Approximate costs for evaluation: $100–$800, depending on the number of tests given
- Approximate costs for counseling/therapy: $80–$100 per hour

Recommendations
- Recommended for both assessment and counseling.

PSYCHIATRIST

Advantages
- trained in differential diagnosis
- able to complete the entire process of assessment and medication management

Disadvantages
- may need to refer for counseling

Costs
- Approximate costs for evaluation: $240–$900, depending on number of sessions
- Approximate costs for therapy: $100–$160 per hour for follow-up sessions

Recommendations
- Recommended for assessment, medical management, possible counseling.

FAMILY PHYSICIAN

Advantages
- familiar with you and your medical history
- relatively inexpensive
- ease of getting appointment

Disadvantages
- limited knowledge, re: differential diagnosis
- needs to refer for counseling
- may need to refer for medical management

Costs
- Approximate costs for evaluation: Same as one or two regular office visits
- Approximate costs for medical management: The number of office visits will vary

Recommendations
- Recommend as first step for medical management following evaluation by mental health professional if trained in this area.
- Generally not recommended for assessment.

NEUROLOGIST

Advantages
- skilled in complex neurological disorders
- able to complete the entire process of assessment and medical management

Disadvantages
- limited knowledge of differential diagnosis
- standard evaluation may include tests that are not necessary for ADD
- will need to refer for counseling

Costs
- Approximate costs for evaluation: $500–$1500 for a full battery of tests

Recommendations
- Recommended in difficult cases in which additional neurological conditions are suspected or known.

MASTER LEVEL COUNSELOR

Advantages
- inexpensive for initial screening
- skilled in individual and group counseling

Disadvantages
- will need to refer for medical management
- will need to refer or consult, re: diagnosis
- limited knowledge of differential diagnosis

Costs
- Approximate costs for counseling/therapy: $60–$90 per hour

Recommendations
- Recommended for counseling for individuals diagnosed with ADD.
- Recommended with reservation to be involved with the initial stages of the assessment process.

SOCIAL WORKER

Advantages
- skilled in psychoanalytic therapy
- inexpensive for initial screening

Disadvantages
- often not skilled in concrete counseling techniques
- limited skills in differential diagnosis
- will need to refer for medical management

Costs
- Approximate costs for therapy: $60–$90 per hour

Recommendations
- Recommended for counseling for individuals diagnosed with ADD with reservations.
- Recommended with reservation to be involved with the initial stages of the assessment process.

All costs listed in this chapter are gathered from an informal sampling of professionals in the Philadelphia area. The costs in your area may be substantially different. We provide these figures for the purpose of general comparison. If you are considering treatment, please make your own cost comparison.

78

Making the Best Choice

In addition to being aware of professional qualifications, you need to be aware of specific training, skills, interests, and expertise that a professional has in the area of ADD. Since adult ADD is a relatively recent discovery, most professionals have not received formal training about it as part of their schooling. It is up to the individual professional to keep abreast of the subject by attending seminars or workshops and reading professional journals and books in the field. Some professionals are more interested in this area and therefore more experienced than others.

If you were to hire someone to clean your house, baby-sit your kids, or fix your car, it would be reasonable to ask for references so you could check out the qualifications of the person you're hiring. When you're hiring someone to help you with mental issues, it makes sense to do the same thing. If you think you might have ADD, you need to make sure the mental health professional you see is qualified to diagnose your disorder and possibly treat it.

Unfortunately, many people have such awe of doctors that they find it difficult to ask questions at all, especially if they are questioning the doctor's abilities. Isn't it rude? Won't the doctor be offended?

No. It's your right to know the qualifications of the doctor or counselor you're considering. They should realize this. However, doctors and counselors are often busy and don't always have time to respond to lengthy questions. So we have prepared a short survey of questions for you to ask.

You don't have to insist on asking the doctor or counselor personally. The office staff should be

79

able to answer these questions over the phone. Or you might mail the questions to the office. (See sample letter that follows.)

After each of the following questions we've left space for you to jot down the answers you receive. Feel free to photocopy the page of questions as often as you need to for your personal use.

FIVE QUESTIONS TO ASK THE PROFESSIONAL

1. Do you see a lot of clients with adult ADD? (How many have you treated over the past year?)

2. How long have you been working with adults with ADD? (Don't be alarmed if the answer is only one or two years. Adult ADD has not been actively diagnosed until the past three to five years. *Do* be concerned if they have only become involved in the past few months.)

3. What is involved in your assessment and treatment process? (Written tests? Interviews? Family history? Behavior modification? Medication?)

4. What are the costs involved?

5. Have you received any special training in the diagnosis or treatment of adult ADD? (Again, don't expect med school or grad school courses. But they may have attended seminars and read widely on the subject.)

SAMPLE LETTER

Date

Your Address

Professional's Address

Dear Dr./Mr./Ms.

I am seeking a professional to provide an evaluation and/or treatment for adult Attention Deficit Disorder. I am aware that many professionals do not yet have expertise or interest in this area. I am hoping you will take a few minutes to help me decide whether or not you have the expertise I am seeking.

1. Approximately how many adults with ADD have you treated over the past year?
___ 0 ___ 1–10 ___ 10–25 ___ 25–50 ___ 50+

2. How long have you been working with adults with ADD?
___ 0–3 months ___ 3–12 months
___ 1–2 years ___ more than 2 years

3. What is involved in your assessment and treatment process?
Assessment
___ clinical interview ___ self-report scales
___ interviews/reports from others ___ IQ testing
___ computer testing ___ other
Treatment
___ counseling ___ behavior management
___ medication ___ other

4. What are the costs involved?

I have enclosed a self-addressed stamped envelope for your convenience. I thank you in advance for your cooperation.

Sincerely,

Your Name

One of the most effective methods of finding those familiar with diagnosing and treating adult ADD in any given area is to contact your local organization for adults with ADD. If you don't know of a local group, contact the following national organizations and ask for information on professionals in your area who might be able to help you.

National ADD Organizations

The Attention Deficit Resource Center
1344 Johnson Ferry Road Suite 14
Marietta, GA 30068
(no phone number available)

ADDA (Attention Deficit Disorder Association)
P.O. Box 2001
West Newbury, MA 01985
(508)462-0495

ANE (Adult Network Exchange)
P.O. Box 1701
Ann Arbor, MI 48106
(313)426-1659

CHADD (Children with Attention Deficit Disorders)
499 NW 70th Avenue Suite 308
Plantation, FL 33317
(305)587-3700

⋆	JUST THE FACTS

Who can diagnose adult ADD?
- a psychologist, psychiatrist, or neurologist
- a master level counselor or social worker (recommended for initial screening only)

(continued)

Please note that the professional must have specific training and expertise in the area of adult ADD. Not all professionals in these categories do. See "Five Questions to Ask the Professional" on page 80.

Seek referrals from adult ADD support organizations. See the list of national organizations on pages 82-83.

Who can medically manage ADD?
- a psychiatrist, a neurologist, or sometimes a family physician

Who can provide counseling for those with ADD?
- a psychologist or Master level counselor
- a psychiatrist or social worker (depending on his or her ability to provide concrete, structured counseling with a problem-solving versus psychoanalytic approach)

Remember that your problems don't all go away once your ADD is discovered and medically treated. There are usually many counseling issues that remain.

CHAPTER SIX

THE ASSESSMENT PROCESS

IN OUR HIGH-TECH society, we look for high-tech gadgetry. So when you're tested for ADD, you want a fancy, plug-in, computer-driven, laser-optic, CD-ROM gizmo to magnetically resonate your ultra-waves and flash the verdict on a backlit, 256-color screen—right?

Wrong.

Nowadays we generally assume that the more technologically advanced a technique is, the better. But when diagnosing ADD, this is not the case. Here's the best technique we have so far:

One person sits in a room telling his or her story to another person.

That's all. No gizmos. Of course, one of those two people should be a mental-health professional trained to recognize ADD. The other is a person, maybe someone like you, who has a history of inattention or hyperactivity or impulsivity. Oh, there's a structured clinical interview format the doctor or counselor might use, and there are self-reports you can fill out. As yet, there is no official test, computer or otherwise, to diagnose ADD.

This fuels the controversy. Without an accepted standard, one doctor may see ADDers behind every rock and another may think the disorder is very rare. As we have seen, two professionals may evaluate the same patient and come to different conclusions due to the absence of objective assessment tools. This has led some in the professional community to question the reality of ADD altogether.

But this really isn't all that unusual. There are other psychological disorders that have no formal "test." In reviewing the *DSM IV*, one can find many other diagnostic categories in which the professional must rely on a clinical interview, observations, and self-report scales to make a diagnosis. There has not been such a fuss regarding the absence of formal "tests" to diagnose depression, anxiety disorders, and adjustment disorders, just to name a few.

We still hope that additional work is done in the area of assessment, with special attention to norm referencing and validity. It would be great to have a reliable ADD test, but in the meantime we must continue to use alternate assessment tools — interviews, self-reports, and differential diagnosis.

But how much assessment do you need? Some professionals have been known to diagnose ADD simply based on a self-report checklist in an office visit of less than ten minutes and at a cost of $30. Other clients have told stories of needing a full two-day extensive workup with a psychologist, social worker, psychiatrist, and neurologist in order to receive the diagnosis at the cost of between $1,500 and $2,000.

What is too much and what is too little? We are faced with a continuum with no visible line marking the "appropriate" amount of diagnostic effort. The extremes are fairly easy to see, but what about the middle ground? How do you know when you're being neglected and when you're being bilked?

Here's what to expect in the process of diagnosing adult ADD.

The Assessment Ingredients

The mental health professional will probably include several pieces when putting together the puzzle of a possible ADD diagnosis. These pieces are usually background information, clinical interview, self-report rating scales, observations of others who know you, a medical examination, and sometimes formal testing. Each piece is important.

BACKGROUND INFORMATION

If you can retrieve your old school records, especially your grades and the teacher comments, this may be extremely helpful to the clinician in helping him or her diagnose ADD. Many times school records include comments such as "not working up to potential," "unable to focus." These comments now are like red flags for diagnosing ADD.

If you have ever been tested for any type of learning or emotional problem, either in school or independently, please obtain copies of the reports prior to your evaluation. This information is also needed to help with an accurate diagnosis.

Be prepared to talk about treatments or strategies you have tried before and their results.

CLINICAL INTERVIEW

As you might expect, you will need to meet personally with the professional who is assessing you for

ADD. The clinical interview will generally take a minimum of two forty-five to fifty minute sessions (two clinical hours), though it might take much longer, depending on individual circumstances.

The doctor or counselor will ask about your current difficulties. Are you having trouble at work or home? Is inattention, hyperactivity, or impulsivity becoming a major problem for you?

But the assessment must also include information about your early childhood history with similar difficulties. Do you remember times of inattention, hyperactivity, or impulsivity as you were growing up? How did friends and family react to you? Did they think you had a problem in one of these areas?

There should also be some type of family history section during this assessment process. A *genogram* (a drawing of your family system) is one useful method to help determine whether or not there might be a family history of ADD or other mental disorders that could impact the diagnosis.

The professional may also ask questions relating to other problems, such as depression, anxiety, learning disabilities, conduct disorders, etc. This is part of the "differential diagnosis," in which he or she tries to rule out alternate explanations for your symptoms.

Clinicians may use informal questions to gather all of this information, or they may rely upon a structured list of questions such as the Barkley Structured Clinical Interview.

SELF-REPORT RATING SCALES

A standard part of most ADD assessments includes some type of rating scale in which you are asked to rate your current behavior on several variables. One example is the Copeland Symptom Checklist for Adult Attention Deficit Disorder.[1]

This type of self-report will help the evaluator have a better idea of the difficulties you now experience that you think might be ADD-related.

You may also be requested to complete an inventory or rating scale regarding your behavior as a child. An example would be the Wender Utah Rating Scale.

It should be noted, however, that the self-reports of many adults with ADD are unreliable because they often over-report or under-report their symptoms, or they don't remember them. Since most adults have "always been this way," it is often difficult for them to have a clear frame of reference in which to evaluate themselves. To further complicate the issue, many have friends and/or family members who also have ADD. So they have a somewhat skewed idea of what is "normal" in these areas.

In addition to the self-report scales for ADD, we have also found it useful to administer the Beck Depression Inventory, since depression often occurs along with ADD.

OBSERVATIONS OF OTHERS

Due to the difficulties with self-observation, it is often helpful to have someone familiar with you also attend a phase of the assessment process. This way the evaluator can get another angle on your situation.

It is also helpful to have parents or siblings complete childhood rating scales regarding what they remember of your childhood.

I (Michele) had one client who had fifteen of his friends fax me copies of his rating scale, all noting very high numbers on many of the ADD characteristics. His parents, on the other hand, only reported observing minimal difficulties for him. It turned out that his parents both probably had ADD and therefore never noticed the symptoms as being out of the ordinary!

FORMAL TESTING

Computer testing. As part of your assessment for ADD, you may be asked to interact with a computer to help assess your ability to focus on a task and follow directions. (Aha! Finally a high-tech gizmo!) At this time, the three major computer diagnostic tools are the Test of Variables of Attention (TOVA), the Continuous Performance Tests (CPT), and The Gordon Diagnostic System.

Although the computer testing may confirm difficulties with attention, there is a tendency for the computers to miss many with ADD (high false-negative rate). This is because persons with ADD tend to perform best in a one-to-one task that is novel and of a short duration. This is exactly the situation created in computer testing. Therefore, such testing is recommended only to add to the information gathered, not to rule out ADD.

IQ testing. You may also be requested to take an individual intelligence test, such as the Wechsler Adult Intelligence Scale (WAIS-R). The purpose of the intelligence test would be to evaluate your overall level of intelligence to help assess whether you really are having difficulty working up to your potential or whether your expectations are unrealistic.

Intelligence testing may also be helpful in some cases to assess for learning disabilities, since many with ADD also have specific learning disabilities.

LEARNING DISABILITIES AND ADD

Although ADD creates difficulty with learning, it is not a formal "learning disability." However, some have estimated that between 50 percent to 80 percent of children and adolescents with ADD will also have a learning disability. Therefore, we can assume that many of the adults who did not "outgrow" ADD still have learning disabilities that may also be affecting their ability to work up to their potential. This is important because the treatments for a learning disability and ADD are not the same, although there is some overlap.

For further information on assessment and treatment of learning disabilities, we recommend two books by Larry Silver. Though written about children, they also relate to adult learning disabilities.

The Misunderstood Child: A Guide for Parents of Children with Learning Disabilities. Larry Silver, M.D., New York: TAB/McGraw-Hill, 1992.

Dr. Larry Silver's Advice to Parents on Attention-Deficit Hyperactivity Disorder. Larry Silver, M.D., Washington D.C.: American Psychiatric Press, 1993.

MEDICAL EXAMINATION

A medical examination is needed to rule out medical conditions that may look like ADD (differential diagnosis again) and to identify any associated disorders that may require medical management. Sometimes ADD-like symptoms can result from an undiagnosed hearing or visual difficulty. Thyroid disorders, although infrequent, may also mimic ADD. Certain seizure disorders may also have similar characteristics.

A medical evaluation will also help determine whether medication is an appropriate form of treatment for you and which medications would work best. For example, if you have high blood pressure or heart difficulties, there are certain ADD medications that you should *not* take.

"The role of the physician in the evaluation of ADHD should not be underestimated," says ADD expert Russell Barkley, "despite overwhelming evidence that by itself the medical exam is inadequate to serve as the basis for a diagnosis of ADHD."[2]

Understanding the Assessment Results
After your assessment, you should be given a report, generally one to three pages. There are three possible results following an ADD assessment:

1. You have ADD.
2. You do not have ADD.
3. It is not certain whether or not the difficulties you are experiencing are due to ADD.

IF YOU HAVE ADD

If you have ADD, the clinician will discuss with you the possible treatment options for its management.

We will present this treatment information in the following chapters.

IF YOU DON'T HAVE ADD

If you do not have ADD, the clinician should recommend further diagnostic testing or other treatments to help with the difficulties you are currently experiencing. Even if it isn't ADD, you still have a problem!

One older adolescent was referred for an ADD evaluation due to her inability to focus, especially on school homework. As it turned out, she did not have ADD but was experiencing emotional difficulties related to interpersonal conflicts. This client participated in individual counseling for a few months and learned to express her feelings rather than stuff them. Her difficulties with concentration disappeared.

IF IT'S NOT CERTAIN

Professionals aren't certain about what to do with the undecided cases. Do you merely try to treat the symptoms through counseling and behavior modification techniques? Or do you go ahead and treat the client medically for ADD on the possibility that ADD is the cause of those symptoms?

If the symptoms are moderate to severe, we recommend the latter course—treating the client as if he or she has ADD. Because medical treatments for ADD are generally quick and therefore easily evaluated, we prefer this approach to the traditional long-term counseling or behavior management approaches.

For example, let's say Jack has trouble paying

attention at work and at home. It has reached the stage where both his job and marriage are in serious trouble. Although he has many ADD symptoms and has had them since childhood, his ADD assessment is inconclusive. He *might* have ADD, but his symptoms might also stem from his ongoing anxiety caused by being raised in a dysfunctional family. The ADD could be causing the anxiety or the anxiety could be causing the ADD symptoms. (The old "Which came first . . .?") We would recommend that first Jack be treated with medication and behavior management for the possible ADD, assuming he has previously tried treatments for anxiety. He will still need counseling regarding the dysfunctional family at a later time, if he has not already addressed this issue. But the ADD treatment is quicker and easier than therapy for anxiety. If it works, Jack's life will begin to change. We've isolated the problem and treated it all at once.

If it doesn't work, we haven't lost much. If Jack does not respond to medication and behavioral treatments, we would then recommend he pursue more in-depth therapy to deal with his unresolved issues.

The alternative would be to treat Jack's anxiety first through therapy. But that could take years and still not yield substantial results—especially if Jack has ADD in addition to the anxiety. By that time, it's likely that Jack will have given up counseling altogether.

If the ADD symptoms are mild, there is no need to rush off to get medical treatment for ADD. Simple behavior management methods could suffice. However, we are not averse to recommending that those with mild ADD also seek medical treatment. You would probably still wear glasses even if

94

you were only mildly nearsighted, wouldn't you?

In summary, we recommend that all the facts be gathered in order to either diagnose or rule out ADD. In cases of uncertain diagnosis, we recommend ruling out ADD through treatment for ADD. If the condition responds to treatment for ADD, it is probably ADD. If not, it's not, and the appropriate treatment program will become more clear. Sometimes, however, even those without ADD respond positively to ADD medication.

JUST THE FACTS

- There is not one conclusive "test" for ADD, but professionals can conduct a thorough assessment.

- The ADD assessment should include background information (school records, previous testing results); a clinical interview (at least two hours long); self-report scales; reports or interviews from others (family, friends); a medical examination; and sometimes formal testing of attention, learning capability, or task performance (computer or IQ).

- When the assessment is inconclusive, we recommend ruling out ADD through treatment of ADD (in moderate to severe cases). If the condition responds to treatment for ADD, it is probably ADD.

NOTES
1. Edna Copeland and Valerie Love, *Attention Please!* (Atlanta: SPI Press, 1991), pp. 323-324.
2. Russell Barkley, Ph.D., *Attention-Deficit Hyperactivity Disorder: A Handbook for Diagnosis and Treatment* (New York: The Guilford Press, 1990), p. 256.

PART THREE

RECOGNIZING THE SYMPTOMS

CHAPTER SEVEN

READY, FIRE, AIM: IMPULSIVITY

MY (Michele's) CLIENT was out driving when he saw a house for sale. Now you must understand that he and his wife were not looking for a house. They had not even discussed the idea of moving. But my client had ADD, with a large measure of impulsivity. And he liked the house.

So he stopped in to take a look. And he bought it.

It won't surprise you that his wife was angry about that. In fact, that marital tension was the main reason he came to see me.

• ◆ •

Ready, Fire, Aim!!!

That's what another client called it—this impulsive quality that affects so many with ADD. His mother always said, "Ready, fire, aim," when she, complained about the reckless things he did. He almost never thought first before he did something, and that continued to create problems for him as an adult. I'm not referring to an occasional impulsive purchase, such as a sweater or electronic gadget that you don't really need. I'm referring to clients who may, on a whim, quit a job, buy an expensive car, or decide to move.

One man I (Michele) counseled had switched jobs over 120 times and was in the process of considering another job change. Another client had moved more than twenty times so far, often for no apparent reason.

Steve had an appointment with a colleague and got there ten minutes early. Impulsively, he knocked on the office door and poked his head in, interrupting a meeting in progress.

"I just wanted to let you know I'm here," he said. "The secretary told me to wait, but I just wanted to let you know I'm here."

You can imagine the nods and glares from the people in that meeting. But five minutes later he knocked again and interrupted the session.

"I just wanted to let you know that I have a hard time waiting," he explained.

Steve has ADD.

• ❖ •

But what's wrong with being spontaneous? Aren't ADD people just "living on the edge" a bit more than the rest of the population, taking chances, breaking the mold, having fun?

One woman with ADD explained the problem to me. Others, she said, may do an occasional impulsive act, but for her it was a lifestyle. For her, control was the exception, impulsivity was the rule. The situations in which she was able to think first and make a rational choice were very few.

"Impulsivity is the second major characteristic

of children with attention disorders," says an expert on childhood ADD. But get this: "Many consider it to be the most serious *and the most enduring* problem in adolescence and adulthood."[1]

A fifteen-year study of children with ADD found that impulsivity was the most pervasive, troublesome, and longstanding of the ADD symptoms.[2]

Hyperactivity in ADD children is often outgrown, or at least rechanneled into more acceptable forms of movement. *Inattention* is a nagging problem for ADD sufferers, but it's largely a private matter and many people can find ways to cope with it. But *impulsiveness* gets you into trouble.

What is impulsiveness? Impulsiveness may refer to:

- actions that are executed too quickly or in an unreasoned way;
- actions that cannot be withheld while deliberations proceed;
- behavior directed in a deliberate fashion toward obtaining immediate gratification at the expense of longer-term goals;
- actions that cannot be stopped or altered once they are initiated, even if the consequences of the action might be undesirable or unpleasant.[3]

Therefore people appear to be impulsive if they respond before they have thought through their desired response or before they have gained an understanding of the task, and if they are less able to stop or alter their actions once started.

A clinical study by Schachar and Tannock (1993) concluded that ADHD is associated with a deficit in *executive control* of action.[4] In other words, the ADD mind is like a company without a CEO, or like a classroom without a teacher. Without that controlling force, things can get chaotic.

The study also found that ADHD is associated with deficits in both *response inhibition* and *response reengagement* processes. That is, the mind lacks the ability to "just say no" to an action once it has thought of it. It's like a car without brakes. Once it gets going, it's hard to stop.

Hallmarks of Impulsivity

DIFFICULTY REACHING LONG-TERM GOALS

Many with ADD find it difficult to engage in the process of working toward long-term goals. Let's say Gail wants to be a teacher, but four years of college seem like an eternity. So she decides to take a job as a secretary. She's earning income from the start, and there's no need for any long-term planning. However, she may become frustrated. She'll be earning less than she could be earning in a job that required advanced training. She'll be working below her potential. All because she made an impulsive, short-term decision to shuck college for the quick money of an immediate job.

SPEAK FIRST, THINK LATER

Impulsivity does not relate just to actions. Adults with ADD often have the most difficulty with their tendency to speak first without thinking about the consequences.

Obviously, this type of impulsivity can create

havoc in interpersonal relationships and careers.

My (Michele's) son, Jarryd, often makes inappropriate statements. He has told me, "I just can't help it. It's like it's connected. An idea comes into my head and it just comes out my mouth. Just one step! There's nowhere to stop it 'cause it's just one step!"

"Just one step." It's that "car without brakes" idea again. You hit the gas pedal and that's it. There's no stopping.

People with ADD often feel a sense of urgency. They *must* share their ideas before they forget or lose the opportunity. They often will interrupt a conversation or blurt out something that has nothing to do with the topic currently being discussed. Since they also have a difficult time evaluating priorities, it is hard for them to differentiate important from unimportant remarks.

LOW FRUSTRATION TOLERANCE

Due to impulsivity, many with ADD have a hard time waiting. This often leads to frustration when the world does not give them what they want when they want it.

In fact, many adults with ADD live their lives in a chronic state of frustration. Little annoyances are magnified. A clerk needs a price check and the person with ADD seethes with impatience. Why? Does he have somewhere to go? Not necessarily— he just can't stand waiting.

ADDers often have a hard time "going with the flow" or being flexible. Experts have suggested that, due to the considerable internal resources needed to compensate for the disorder, ADDers are "used up" and therefore don't have the additional resources needed to deal with these "extra" situations.

SHIFTING FROM TASK TO TASK

Another byproduct of impulsivity is difficulty completing tasks. Many with ADD find it very hard to resist the urge to do something else, especially if they are engaged in a task they're not crazy about.

When Janet* was asked whether any of her family members might have ADD, she laughed and said, "I know my mother had it! She even won an award for having the most unfinished craft projects, and she only showed a portion of them. She always had good intentions but somehow never finished anything. Her life was sidetracked."

Dan*, another ADD client, also had difficulty finishing things. Once I (Michele) was interviewing him with his wife, Carol, who listed the household projects he had started but never completed.

"The worst one," she said, "is the wall he knocked down, intending to put up a new one. That was three weeks ago, and the new wall isn't up yet. It's still just a pile of rubble."

"Oh," I said.

"You don't understand," Carol replied. "It's an outside wall!"

• ◆ •

RIGID OR COMPULSIVE
COPING STRATEGIES

Some ADDers may have developed a very rigid sense of structure in order to manage their impulsive behavior. One client, for example, who has become a Marine, finds there the external structure and discipline he lacks internally.

We know one man who is a relentless list-maker. Each day he makes a long list of "things to do," far too long to be completed. There are so many things he wants and needs to do, so he tries to corral them all on paper. Every year he buys at least one schedule book or "personal organizer," but he seldom stays with it through January. Still, his listmaking puts some structure in his life. It's one way of coping with his impulsive tendencies.

The internal filter that processes decisions seems to be impaired with some types of ADD. If this is a problem for you, try the following strategies.

FIVE TIPS FOR CURBING IMPULSIVITY

1. Take time to "aim." Can you relate too well to the Ready, Fire, Aim image? If so take time to "Aim" first through the use of a slogan, mental image, or visual cue to prompt you to think first. Some have learned "count to ten" before expressing anger. Perhaps you could do something similar before acting rashly on some new thought.

2. Elicit the feedback of others. As a reality check, consult with others, who do not have ADD, before making a major decision.

3. Don't have a lot of money with you. Many sufferers of ADD find it helpful not to have large sums of cash, a charge card, or a checkbook on their person. That way, if an item in a store tempts them, they won't have the means to act on the temptation. By the time they go home for the money, often they no longer have a desire for the item.

4. Tell close friends about your struggle. Confide in close friends and coworkers about your ADD. Give them permission to be brutally honest with you if you are doing or saying something out of line. (Then, when they are honest, accept the feedback and try to make amends.)

5. If you are not getting treatment for ADD, seek it. A counselor should be able to help devise coping strategies for your impulsive tendencies, and medication could also help.

JUST THE FACTS

- Impulsiveness is a frequent component of ADD behavior.

- Impulsiveness includes:

  Acting hastily or recklessly

  Inability to stop actions once started

  Difficulty pursuing long-term goals

  Speaking inappropriately

  Inability to wait without becoming highly frustrated

  Shifting from task to task

  Rigid or compulsive coping strategies

- Impulsivity can be effectively curbed with a few simple strategies.

NOTES
1. Edna Copeland and Valerie Love, *Attention, Please!* (Atlanta, GA: SPI Press, 1991), p. 30.
2. G. Weiss and L. T. Hechtman, *Hyperactive Children Grown Up* (New York: Guilford Press, 1986); G. Weiss, L. Hechtman, T. Milroy, T. Perlman, "Psychiatric Status of Hyperactives as Adults: A Controlled Prospective 15-Year Follow-Up of 63 Hyperactive Children," *Journal of American Academy of Child Psychiatry* (1985), pp. 211-220.
3. Russell Schachar and Rosemary Tannock, "Inhibitory Control, Impulsivity, and Attention Deficit Hyperactivity Disorder," *Clinical Psychology Review*, vol. 13 (1993), pp. 721-739.
4. Schachar and Tannock, pp. 721-739.

CHAPTER EIGHT

DANCING TO A FASTER DRUMMER: HYPERACTIVITY

MARIA IS A BUNDLE of energy. She has a warm smile and a bubbly personality—and she can't sit still. She never could.

Growing up with four brothers, Maria learned to climb trees and play football. Her family figured she was just a tomboy, but she was always on the go.

She went to a Catholic school and even there she couldn't sit still. The nuns would offer her rewards to sit and pay attention, but her mind and body were always going twice as fast as the rest of the class. Maria found herself withdrawing from her classmates. She just danced to a faster drummer.

In college, Maria set her sights on the medical profession, but she couldn't get through the pre-med courses. She was bright enough, but her mind would go racing elsewhere while she was studying or listening to a lecture. As a result, she knew some aspects of those subjects very well but had huge gaps in her knowledge. Maria had to switch her major to physical education.

Eventually, Maria got work in a hospital's physical therapy center, a job in which her physical hyperactivity could actually help her. She maintained an interest in fitness, running six miles a day. She married a man who was very patient and supportive. But she was still frustrated.

"Your self-esteem's always on the floor," Maria says, "because you see everybody rising to the top and you know you could do the same thing and probably better." All her attempts at education and advancement seemed to fail.

Then an article in a magazine caught her eye. It was about Attention Deficit Disorder. The symptoms described in the magazine matched Maria perfectly. Maybe there was an answer to her problems.

Maria was shy, however, about claiming this disorder as her own. "At first," she says, "I was afraid people would think I was stupid, an idiot, which I'm not! I was afraid they would reject me, that I would lose friends, that they'd look at me like I was a psycho." Unlike those who eagerly accept an ADD diagnosis as an explanation for their mysterious woes, Maria wanted to deny it at first. She was embarrassed by the thought that there might be something "wrong" with her brain.

It took two years of wrestling with the idea before Maria finally did something about it. She saw an article in a local newspaper about an ADD seminar sponsored by our counseling office. She put it off. Then she saw a second article and decided to come in to see me (Michele).

With some trepidation, she arrived for the initial interview. "I could hear every single noise in the office," she says. "I could hear the clock ticking. I could hear people whispering. Anything like that."

As she described her experiences, she seemed like a good candidate for ADD. She spoke rapidly, darting off to one subject, then another. Despite her nervousness, she was blurting things out with a delightful honesty. I also saw the hyperactivity in her fidgeting hands and tapping feet. In addition, her story of lost potential, disorganization, unbridled emotions, and general frustration was classic ADD.

I referred Maria to a psychiatrist who prescribed medication—Ritalin. She returned to me regularly for counseling and joined a group of ADDers for mutual support and sharing.

Shortly after beginning treatment, Maria went back to school for a degree in physical therapy. She found it impossible to take a full course load and keep her job and tend to her family. But now she has cut down on her course work. "It's frustrating," she says. "A degree that should take two years is taking me three years, but I'll get there."

Maria is choosing to manage her ADD by taking her medication only when she absolutely needs it—to study for class or to get through a potentially explosive time at work. "With the Ritalin, it gives you focus," she explains. "It helps you to say, 'All right, today I'm going to do this, this, and this.'

"And through the counseling, I'm learning to prioritize. You see, we ADDers have no concept of priorities, organization, when to call when you're late, when to keep quiet when you're really angry. Counseling helps us learn those things."

Maria's still a bundle of energy. And there are times when her hyperactivity works for her, making her energetic, exciting, inspiring, and fun to be with. But now she knows how to focus when she must.

• ◆ •

Hyperactivity was one of the first conditions associated with ADD. That's why the clinical name for the problem is ADHD—Attention Deficit *Hyperactive* Disorder. (More recently, our understanding of ADD has expanded to include those without hyperactivity. Some adults with ADD are hyperactive and some are not.)

Adults with hyperactive ADD have a history of hyperactive behavior as children. In most cases, the childhood hyperactivity was much greater than the person's current hyperactive behavior. Either adults gradually learn some control strategies, or they just don't have as much energy as they did before. (In a few cases, where children were threatened with severe punishment for hyperactive movement, they actually display *more* hyperactivity as they enter adulthood.)

What Hyperactivity Looks Like

Most adults have signs of fidgety behavior rather than the gross (large) motor movements more common of hyperactive children. Although inside they may want to be in constant or at least frequent motion, by the time they have reached adulthood, most adults have managed to contain or suppress the hyperactive component of ADD. The remaining signs are usually frequent changes in seat position, frequent crossing and uncrossing of arms or legs, movements of the foot or fingers, such as tapping.

To be less clinical—squirming and squiggling.

Rapid or excessive talking may also be a sign of hyperactivity in adults. "Motor mouth" may be a nickname.

Hyperactivity is frequently misunderstood in adults. While people in general tend to accept hyperactive children, smiling wryly and feeling sorry for the parents, hyperactive adults seldom get the same leeway. Because adults have often learned to manage their hyperactivity *to some degree*, their occasional outbursts of movement are often judged as willful and inconsiderate.

Fortunately, many adult ADDers are able to turn their endless energy into successful businesses. They can be tireless workers in community efforts and volunteer organizations, and often they're great with young people. Many become self-employed to allow themselves the ability to utilize their strengths and hire others to compensate for their weaknesses.

The Continuum
The physical signs and symptoms of hyperactivity are easiest to see in extremes. One ADD client, for example, was constantly pacing around my (Michele's) office during our initial fifty-minute session, and even left the room three times. Many hyperactive adults find it difficult to stay seated for longer than ten minutes without getting up to move around.

But how does hyperactivity differ from merely "high" activity? It's easy to see the difference between a hyperactive adult and, say, a couch potato. But what about the high-powered, Type A executive who rushes from meeting to meeting? Or the person who is merely nervous or dealing with stress?

113

What makes hyperactivity hyper?

There's a continuum here. If we could go to a mall and line up one hundred people in order of hyperactive-fidgety behavior, we would find a wide range.

At one end would be the sloths, trudging from store to store, barely putting one foot in front of the other. (And presumably there's a group of people at home too listless to go to the mall.)

Toward the middle of our lineup would be those with "normal" energy. They have moved at a medium pace through the mall, and perhaps visited five or six stores.

At the high end we have the bumblebees, flitting from one store to the next, picking up this object and that one, going back and forth to check prices, racing through the food court.

Now, how many of these are hyperactive, and how many just have a lot to do? And where do you fit in? Are you more fidgety than ninety of these people in our mall lineup? Ninety-five? Ninety-nine?

But our evaluation goes beyond mere percentiles. The key question is this: *Is it interfering with your life?* Are there things you cannot do because of hyperactivity? Are there concerts or movies you would like to sit through, but just can't? Are your relationships suffering because you can't engage in lengthy conversations? Is it difficult for you to keep a job because you can't seem to stay at your assigned post?

Hyperactive ADD and Type A Behavior

Often in response to societal demands, a person may feel stressed and pressured to work quicker and accomplish more. As a result, a hard-driving Type A person without ADD can often look very similar to an ADDer. But the hyperactive, impulsive behavior associated with ADD is different from the hurried, rushed style of Type A behavior in both origin and intent.

A person described as a Type A personality seems to live life in a continual sense of urgency. Life is a giant pressure cooker. The Type A person has to respond quickly to situations that arise. He or she will often feel anxious, impatient, frustrated.

How does such a person respond to the increasing pressure of new information and rapid change? *By speeding up.* Robert and Marilyn Kriegel explain it this way: "The harried individual trying to keep up with these changes talks fast, walks fast, and acts as if slowing down to relax is tantamount to failure. Life is a continual race against the clock.

"The irony is that, while many Type A's use achievement to justify their behavior, they don't perform nearly as well as they could. They become hyperactive, and rush around trying to do too much, too quickly, and as a result accomplish little of quality."[1]

Some of the same dynamics occur in hyperactive ADDers. Yet there are distinct differences that need to be distinguished during a complete ADD assessment.

In order to have ADD, there needs to be a *prior history* of impulsive and/or hyperactive acts. Most Type A adults adopt those habits in adulthood in response to job or family pressures.

In order to have ADD, these characteristics need to *cross all settings.* Type A people can often be mellow in family settings or while on vacation, whereas an ADDer cannot turn off his or her hyperactivity.

115

FIVE TIPS FOR CURBING HYPERACTIVITY

1. Physical exercise is very important in reducing the feelings of uncontrolled hyperactivity. You may need to take several short exercise breaks throughout the day.

2. Short breaks for rest and relaxation may help someone with ADD to settle enough to remain on task and in the room they need to remain in. (This is also a good idea for Type A personalities.)

3. Mental relaxation breaks can also help, since an ADDer's hyperactive body is usually accompanied by a hyperactive mind. Take deep breaths and visualize a restful scene. (For some that might be a quiet beach, but others might "expend" some of their surplus energy by envisioning themselves running a marathon.)

4. The calming techniques of Yoga may also be of interest to some.

5. Medication is frequently helpful if behavior modification techniques fail. Many clients report the most significant improvement in their hyperactivity in response to medication management.

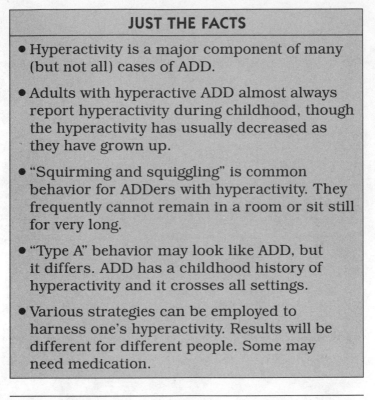

JUST THE FACTS

- Hyperactivity is a major component of many (but not all) cases of ADD.

- Adults with hyperactive ADD almost always report hyperactivity during childhood, though the hyperactivity has usually decreased as they have grown up.

- "Squirming and squiggling" is common behavior for ADDers with hyperactivity. They frequently cannot remain in a room or sit still for very long.

- "Type A" behavior may look like ADD, but it differs. ADD has a childhood history of hyperactivity and it crosses all settings.

- Various strategies can be employed to harness one's hyperactivity. Results will be different for different people. Some may need medication.

NOTE
1. Robert Kriegel, Ph.D., and Marilyn Kriegel, Ph.D., *The C Zone: Peak Performance Under Pressure* (New York: Fawcett Columbine, 1984), p. xiv.

117

CHAPTER NINE

CHANNEL SURFING: INATTENTION

"I CAN'T EVEN STAY focused on my daydreams!" one ADD client said. "I have daydreams within my daydreams! I can be trying to focus on a presentation at work when I start to daydream. Before I know it, I'm off into another daydream. Sometimes I can have four or five sub-daydreams within my one daydream. All this while I'm trying to pay attention to a presentation at work. It's very frustrating!"

Living with ADD is like watching television with a channel surfer. A few seconds of one station followed by a few minutes of another followed by a few seconds of several stations. . . .

The major symptom of Attention Deficit Disorder is, as you might guess, a lack of attention. This does not mean that ADDers can never pay attention to anything, it means they have a deficit. That is, they cannot pay attention as much, as often, or as consistently as others.

Many characteristics of ADD vary, such as hyperactivity, which may or may not be present. But nearly every adult with ADD has problems with inattention, an inability to concentrate consistently on important tasks or stimuli.

This lack of consistency can be maddening for people with ADD. Generally they can get most of the facts in a given situation, but this can be even more frustrating than missing the whole picture. If you know you have no clue about something, you'll ask about it, or you'll avoid situations where you'll need to know these facts. But a person with ADD often doesn't know what's missing.

For example, a wife tells her ADD husband, "Tonight my last business client is at 4:30. I'll be home after 6:00. I'll bring home pizza for dinner." The husband, however, hears, "Tonight my last client . . . 4:30 . . . I'll bring home pizza for dinner." So when his wife comes home at 6:30 with the pizza, he's upset. He has been waiting for two hours! The wife is frustrated because she's being blamed for something she never said she would do.

Similarly, a student with ADD may read the assigned textbook chapter and expect to do well on a test. Imagine her surprise when the questions cover something she has totally missed! Yes, she read the chapter, but her attention drifted away at certain points.

We hear a regular refrain from ADDers who have underachieved in school. They may be quite intelligent, but they cannot study effectively, and so they often fail. Their mental picture of things is something like a slice of Swiss cheese with holes here and there.

> "I can't even stay   daydreams! one ADD
>   have daydreams within my   trying
> to focus on a presentation at work when I start
> Before I know it, I'm off   Sometimes I
> can have four or   within my one daydream.

120

All trying to pay attention to a presentation at work. It's very
          like watching TV with a channel surf one station, followed by a few   another,
followed by a few several stations. . . .
          of Attention Deficit Disorder
guess, a lack of attention. This does not mean that ADDers can *never* pay attention to
they have a deficit. That is,   pay

When a person with ADD reads a page in a book, the information received may "look" like the text above. That's because their attention may fade in and out. While this section depicts two-thirds of the information of the previous page, obviously it's nearly impossible to make sense of it.

This is life with ADD—getting most or some of the facts, but always needing to fill in the gaps. Some ADDers become quite adept at guessing what they've missed and faking their way through life, but it's a tough game to play, and sometimes they get caught. This can be embarrassing and frustrating.

Sometimes parents, friends, and teachers can misread ADD in an intelligent person. Maria tells of a professor who would not believe she had ADD. The professor saw ADD as a learning disability or a kind of mental retardation. Because Maria was often very perceptive in class, learning some things quite well, the professor figured she was just making excuses. But ADD is not an *inability* to concentrate, but an *inconsistency* of concentration. These lapses of concentration create difficulties with memory, organization, interpersonal relationships, and career success.

121

The inconsistent attention of the ADDer means that one day a household task will get done and the next day it won't; one day an appointment will be remembered and the next day it will be missed. Teachers, employers, and family members who don't understand ADD can easily assume that the ADDer is just being obstinate, uncooperative, passive-aggressive, or lazy. "You did this yesterday! Why not today?" Even those who do understand ADD can be extremely frustrated with the ADDer's erratic behavior.

Blinks

James Reisinger, who has ADD himself, has written a booklet in which he refers to an ADDer's lapses in concentration as "blinks."[1] It's a helpful concept.

Everyone blinks. We close our eyes often, for a split-second at a time. But what if you blinked and didn't open your eyes for five seconds or twenty seconds or a full minute? What if you opened your eyes after a long blink and didn't know you had missed anything? That would be similar to the everyday experience of a person with ADD.

A friend of ours (without ADD) has a habit of falling asleep while watching movies on video. He'll rent a tape and watch it late at night when he's dead-tired. He tells us he has "sort of" watched a lot of great movies. This guy is a perfect picture of the "blink" theory. As his eyelids grow heavy, he literally blinks and keeps his eyes closed, drifting into sleep for ten or fifteen minutes. When he opens his eyes, he doesn't realize how much of the movie he's missed. He thinks he's watching the next scene, but he's actually missed five or six major scenes of the movie. Suddenly the characters are talking about things he doesn't know anything about. He has to piece together the plot, but then he drifts off again and misses more. As the closing credits roll, he thinks he has seen 95 percent of a disjointed film, but his wife tells him he was snoring through a third of it.

Similarly, the ADDer generally has no idea how much action he or she has missed. People with ADD are always trying to "piece together the plot" of what's happening around them. As one successful businessman explained, "I have developed systems of dealing with things based on incomplete information. I'm not sure when I've had a skip [blink], I just find out that I have missed things all the time."[2]

Like normal blinking, an ADDer's distractions are completely involuntary. They just seem to come. But unlike our friend watching late movies, the ADDer does not drift off into the nothingness of sleep. On the contrary, the ADDer's "blink" is filled with mental activity—"thoughts, images, memories, plans, or calculations that are often totally unrelated to the subject at hand," says Reisinger.[3]

"The ADDer's mind seems to have a dozen open channels to every thought, sound, or sight," Reisinger adds. "Thoughts spring from one to another and then wander on."[4]

For this reason, ADDers tend to be very creative people. Their minds are filled with exciting images, bold metaphors, new ways of doing things. Several clients have told us they occasionally stop taking their medication when they need to be creative. They need to let their minds fly free for a while.

Of course the difficulty comes when there's a job to do, a person to see, a meeting to remember, a bill to pay. The ADDer finds it hard to stay focused on the mundane activities of daily life.

Concentration difficulties also escalate with boredom and fatigue. If an ADDer is working on a familiar task, there is an increased tendency to daydream. Or if an ADDer has been focusing on some task for a period of time, he or she may "use up" the supply of concentration and may have difficulty with the next project or task. Concentration is "expensive" for a person with ADD.

What We're Up Against

We see several aspects of attention deficit in ADDers.

Internal distractibility. Thoughts keep popping into their heads. You might call this "mental hyperactivity"—the mind is always on the go. If an ADDer is listening to a lecture, any word may spin off a series of puns, images, memories, or theories.

External distractibility. Noises get them off-track. So will movements they see with their peripheral vision. The ADDer's power of observation can be quite remarkable. Once I (Michele) was in a restaurant with my family and I could tell my son Jarryd, who has ADD, was highly distracted. I asked him, "What do you hear?" He proceeded to provide an amazingly thorough list of all the noises in the restaurant. The people talking in the corner. The dishes clinking in the kitchen. The fork scratching the plate at the next table. The waiter's footsteps. Unable to filter out all these sounds, he naturally found it difficult to focus on the conversation at *our* table.

Inability to "weigh" data. In writing a book like this, we have a lot of information available, but we have to sort through it. We have to decide what's more important and what's less important. We have to "weigh" the data available to determine which items are worth our (and your) attention. The ADDer has difficulty weighing the merits of different input. Jarryd in the restaurant was hearing a cacophony of sound, but he lacked the ability to sort it. Non-ADDers have little problem in saying, "That conversation across the room is not as important as the one at this table." ADDers find it hard to make that judgment.

Disinhibition. You may have heard the Broadway song "I'm Just a Girl Who Can't Say No." ADDers have a similar situation. It's what some researchers call disinhibition. At times, ADDers lose their ability to reject certain thoughts or actions. They are receiving sensory input and their minds are churning out auxiliary thoughts, and they can't say no to any of it. They follow each sound or thought as it comes, because they are unable to put it in its place.

Components of Inattention

The various components of inattention can be defined as difficulty in the following:

- Choosing the item to focus on.
- Ability to keep paying attention.
- Paying attention to more than one item or thought.
- Stopping attention to one task to shift to another task.

We can see that the lack of "weighing" ability might keep an ADDer from *choosing the right stimulus* to focus on. Distractibility, external and internal, continually battles with an ADDer's efforts to *sustain the focus over time.* The other two components *(dividing the focus* and *shifting focus)* have to do with transitions. Even when an ADDer succeeds at staying focused on one task, the switch to another task can be devastating.

Say a woman with ADD is strolling with her husband. He gazes at the horizon and says, "Look at that sunset. Isn't that gorgeous? It reminds me of our first date. Do you remember?"

The wife says, "Remember what?"

The problem is that the husband is asking her to *divide her attention.* She may have been fine as they strolled, working hard to keep her attention on him as they talked. But then he directed her attention to the sunset, and then to their first date, and she couldn't handle the transition. She could look at the sunset or listen to him, but she couldn't do both.

ADDers regularly "groove in" to certain tasks, but if they're interrupted, it's hard to get back to what they were doing. A man with ADD may be successfully screening out distractions and typing up a report, but if the phone rings and he answers it, he'll forget about the report. ADDers find it difficult to *shift from one stimulus to another.* Transitions of attention are the most vulnerable times for those with ADD.

With that in mind, we must say that this is a difficult time for ADDers to live in. This is a fast-paced age. MTV has revolutionized entertainment by changing visual images every few seconds. Distractions abound and transitions are many. In fact, this may be why adult ADD has just come to the surface as a widespread disorder. In slower times, people could cope much better. The battle to control their attention was not as fierce. But now anyone who cannot keep up with our go-go culture gets left behind. It becomes more obvious that there's a problem.

"Paying attention" is something non-ADDers take for granted, but it's an ongoing struggle for those with ADD. As we have seen, it means:

1. A person must find the appropriate stimulus and focus on it.
2. The person must sustain focus.
3. When appropriate, the person must release this focus so that he or she can move to another stimulus.

Each of these steps is difficult for the person with ADD.

Other Causes of Inattention

People with a high degree of *anxiety* often find it hard to concentrate. They may be distracted from everyday tasks in much the same way as those with ADD. What's the difference?

Primarily, anxiety is a *temporary* condition. Those who are anxious generally have been able to concentrate in the past. Their current distractibility is a reaction to certain temporary pressures. However, ADDers have a lifelong history of attention deficit.

Anxiety is also *limited*, in most cases. That is, it tends to occur in only one or two areas of life. That is, a man may be anxious about his job performance, and so he has difficulty remembering details or focusing on a task at work. Perhaps some of that anxiety even carries over to his home life. But put him on a Caribbean beach and the anxiety dissipates along with the distractibility. An

ADDer on a Caribbean beach will still have trouble focusing consistently.

Depression also creates distractibility and can be as pervasive as ADD, affecting all areas of life. But again, ADD is distinctly a lifelong disorder. With a thorough case history and differential diagnosis, a professional can determine whether one's lack of consistent attention is caused by ADD or depression, or some other disorder.

Ramifications of Attention Deficit

One study tested ADDers in their ability to attend to and complete a task. It found that their performance goes up and down (refer to graph below). Sometimes they can attend to a task even *better* than those without ADD, but much of the time their attention is far worse.

PERCENTAGE WORK COMPLETED[5]

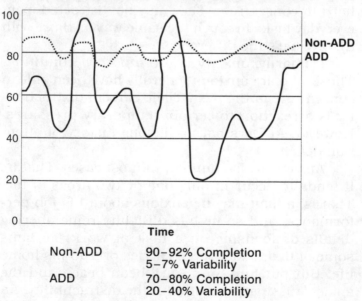

Non-ADD	90–92% Completion
	5–7% Variability
ADD	70–80% Completion
	20–40% Variability

Because of all that "down time," the researcher concludes, it takes ADDers *three to four times longer* to complete tasks.

Remember Helen's daughter, Laura, a high school student who has ADD? Laura tells of times she studied all night for a test and still didn't do as well as her friends who cracked the books for maybe an hour. This is a common complaint of ADDers, who have to work doubly hard (and then some!) to get their work done.

When you consider the cumulative effect of education, the problem becomes even more acute. If a young child was distracted while the class was learning p's and q's, how will he learn to read? He may know 92 percent of the alphabet, but he'll stumble on a lot of words. If a child is "blinking" while the class studies subtraction, how will she ever understand long division?

Because of their increased "down time," ADD students are always catching up. They learn to make assumptions, to guess at what they missed, and they can be pretty clever about this. But they still find it hard to master any subject.

The same difficulties can be seen *on the job.* In business, people often talk about a "learning curve." It takes a new employee a certain amount of time to master a task. But the curve is greatly altered for a person with ADD who can learn aspects of the assignment very quickly but miss key instructions.

So, should ADDers stick to easy, nonchallenging jobs? Not at all! The boredom factor can often yield even greater distractibility. And there's no reason that ADDers can't be helped to live up to their full potential.

There are also many problems, major and

minor, that arise from attention deficit *in daily life*. Imagine how many hours are lost by ADDers looking for their keys or for their tax forms.

Assets of Attention Deficit

As we have said, the same factors that send ADDers' minds chasing after distractions also help them to think creatively. The disinhibition that creates some embarrassing social situations can also create some rather stunning art. Non-ADDers tend to restrict their thinking to certain "normal," acceptable, predictable patterns. The ADDer usually breaks through those patterns.

This wide-eyed perspective is not only good for painters and poets, but also for entrepreneurs. The creative thinking that comes with ADD can be an asset for high-level executives—if they can find a way to get through the paperwork. Often they have secretaries or friends or spouses who keep them organized while they keep churning out creative ideas.

Because ADDers' senses do not focus tightly on subjects, they are more apt to get the big picture of what's going on. ADDers can be very observant. At a party, the non-ADDer may engage in a few great conversations, but the ADDer will probably also notice what everyone is wearing, who's talking to whom, and how often the punch bowl is filled.

I (Michele) see this "full view of life" in my son, Jarryd, on a regular basis. For example, while working on a school assignment at the kitchen table, he will see through the window a red-headed woodpecker, six blue jays, and the beautiful pink sunset. All these things I would have missed, even though I was washing the dishes in the same kitchen at the same time. Because I was focused solely on my task, I would not have seen the sky or the birds.

One of my clients is an inspector of plant operations. He is very good at his job because he sees everything. Nothing escapes his full view of the world. On one visit to my office he said, "You know, the left rear tire on your car looks pretty low. You ought to get that checked." When I took the car to the shop, sure enough, there was a small leak. Only a person with ADD would notice a small amount of air missing from a tire of a car over fifty yards away, which he passed on the way to an appointment!

SIX TIPS TO IMPROVE ATTENTION

1. Battle boredom. Boredom is a deterrent to attention. That's true for people with and without ADD. But if you have ADD, it is practically impossible to stay with a boring task.

So do what you can to make tasks less boring. Obviously, this is easier said than done, but you can try to inject humor whenever possible, add drama and suspense to mundane activities, use bright colors, and do tasks in new ways.

2. Reward success. Rewards offered for the successful completion of tasks is a basic element of behavior management. If highly motivated, an ADDer may be able to focus better. That act of focusing is still "expensive" —it uses up a lot of energy—so you may

(continued)

want to reward yourself with a mental "vacation" for a certain amount of time. But be sure to play by the rules. Do not reward yourself when you're "almost" finished; press for the actual completion of the task.

3. Put up "signposts." The distracted mind goes wandering over unmapped boulevards. You need to put up "signposts" so you can find your way back to the task at hand. The classic "signpost" is the string tied around a finger to keep you from forgetting something. People put up signs on their mirrors, on their refrigerators, on their car dashboards—"Don't forget this!" Other people make lists of things to do. We keep telling ADD people to *write things down* (especially appointment times with us!).

4. Simplify your space. If constant distraction is a problem for you, do not put your desk by a window; face the wall. Do not listen to a news radio station as you work; try a station with monotonous music (such music can help to mask extraneous office noise). Do not put a million things on your walls that might draw your mind away from the task at hand. Keep things simple in your work space.

This is actually a complex point, because some ADDers *need* a stimulating environment. They get distracted if an office is *too* quiet. Know yourself. Know what works for you, and set up your space accordingly.

(continued)

5. Stop beating yourself up. Stop beating yourself up emotionally, that is. Many ADDers will attempt a task and then go off on a mental journey of distractions. When they come back to the task, they are full of self-recrimination. "I am so bad. Look at all this time I wasted. I have no self-discipline. I couldn't even do this little thing. Now I'm so far behind." This kind of negative self-talk can actually be a disincentive. You're like the runaway child who finally wants to return home but fears punishment. If your runaway mind expects to receive insults when it finally comes back to the task, it may stay out there a little longer. Change your self-talk. Accept the fact that you are easily distracted. Applaud your own creativity. Jot down new ideas that arise from your mental wanderings. Set reasonable goals for your work, allowing for some "distraction time."

6. Consider medication. For some people with ADD, all the behavior modification methods in the world won't do much good. There are ADDers who have stacks of Day-Timers, who work with bare walls and nonstop Muzak, who promise themselves trips to Tahiti if they'd only get the job done — and still they don't get the job done. When it comes right down to it, ADD involves a glitch in the electrical circuitry of the brain. You can't behavior-manage that! But in conjunction with counseling and behavior management, medication can help immensely.

JUST THE FACTS

- The hallmark of ADD is *inconsistent* attention, rather than the inability to concentrate at all.

- We can think of ADD distractions as "blinks," in which a person misses certain pieces of what's going on (but is active in a mental journey of his or her own). This results in a "Swiss-cheese" view of life, full of holes, making it three or four times as hard to keep up in school or work. Many ADDers find success by figuring out or guessing what goes in those gaps.

- Inattention consists of an inability to focus on the proper subject, sustain that focus, split that focus between two subjects, or make a transition to a new subject. ADDers have trouble in all those areas.

- ADDers face external distractions of sight and sound, as well as internal distractions of thoughts that are sparked by words or images. They usually have difficulty weighing the importance of what they perceive and tend to say yes to every new stimulus (disinhibition), rather than filtering out unimportant material.

- There are also many positive characteristics of ADD, notably, creativity and a "full view of life."

- ADDers can use various behavior-modification and psychological techniques to improve their attention, but they should also consider medication.

NOTES

1. James Reisinger, *BLINKS: A Phenomenon of Distractibility in Attention Deficit Disorder*, P.O. Box 1701, Ann Arbor, MI 48106.
2. Quoted by James Reisinger, in "Blinks," *Parents Supporting Parents*, p. 6 (article condensed by Margie Shankin from Reisinger's booklet).
3. Reisinger, p. 5.
4. Reisinger, p. 5.
5. Keith Bauer, *Attention Deficit Hyperactivity Disorder in Children and Adolescents* (Milwaukee, WI: Professional Educational Resources, 1993), p. 5, graph on p. 49.

PART FOUR

EXPLORING TREATMENT OPTIONS

CHAPTER TEN

MEDICATION

LET ME (MICHELE) TELL *you about my son,*
Jarryd. He is a delight, but he's also a handful.
I could fill this book with stories of his adven-
tures, but I'll limit myself to a few highlights.

There was the time he jumped through the
living room window and landed outside in some
bushes. Once he saw some pennies in a reflect-
ing pool at the mall and jumped in to get them.
He wore out the staff at six different daycare
centers before the age of five. My husband and
I found it difficult to take him shopping with us,
or to church, or out to eat, because of his disrup-
tive behavior. We've been asked to leave stores
because of him.

I am a psychologist with an emphasis in
behavior modification. Surely I could find a way
to modify my own son! We tried various reinforce-
ment and consequence contingencies to no avail.
Our methods made absolutely no difference!
Oh, Jarryd also was always sorry and regretful.
He's not a bad kid. He did not enjoy getting into
trouble, he said he just couldn't help it.

On one trip to the pediatrician for a routine
evaluation, Jarryd escaped from the office and
ran down the hallway at least five times in less
than ten minutes, disrupting medical supplies
and ripping the paper that covered examination
tables. He just would not sit still.

The doctor knew that these behaviors were
routine for Jarryd, and asked if we had thought
of giving him medication. I was a little surprised
that a doctor would make such an offhand
recommendation without a thorough screening
and diagnosis.

A similar thing happened later with a neurologist who was evaluating Jarryd for a possible
seizure disorder. Once again, with no more
than a quick look, he had suggested medication
management for ADD. All Jarryd had done was,
once again, leave the office and run down the
hall several times, crawl under the desk, almost
rip the curtains down and refuse to stay still for
an evaluation. But I was taken aback by the fact
that two doctors were so freely peddling their
medications.

In retrospect, I think the doctors knew something I did not. Even though I knew that Jarryd
had ADD from a very early age, I felt that his
misbehavior should be able to be controlled
through behavior and environment management.
After all, that was my specialty.

But behavioral methods weren't working.
These doctors knew that the medication could
help Jarryd's brain to function properly. They
could tell, even from brief observation, that he
was highly impulsive, hyperactive and extremely
distractible — a very likely candidate for medical
intervention. At the time, I felt that they were

merely trying to sedate my child, and so I resisted.

Through my entire career, I had been skeptical of medical intervention for inattention difficulties. Given the information available to me at the time, it seemed that the difficulties were not physiological but more due to poor parenting, poor teacher discipline techniques, or lack of motivation on the part of capable students who were not working up to their potential. With proper rewards and penalties, organizational techniques, and a proper understanding of the issues, these students could overcome their difficulties, I was sure of it. Some did. But others failed repeatedly. When they did, I just assumed that someone — teachers, parents, or the students themselves — stopped trying.

But I saw my son trying desperately to "be good," and failing again and again. This was not only threatening everything I believed in, professionally — it was breaking my heart.

Then I saw pictures of the brain from studies conducted by the National Institute of Mental Health on ADD, which indicate that the brain of a person with ADD is physically different from the brain of a person without it. ADD is not an emotional disorder or a result of bad learning. There is just some unusual wiring in the brain! The transmitters are not transmitting properly. It is a physiological problem — and it can possibly be set right with medication to get those transmitters working again.

We tried medication with Jarryd and saw tremendous results. It's not a cure-all. There's still a good bit of behavior management required. But Jarryd is now able to respond to behavioral techniques. Under medication, he is able to control himself. He can be the good kid he wants to be.

This whole experience has led me to a kind of conversion. I did a 180-degree turn and suddenly became an ardent supporter of medication as a piece of the treatment package for ADD. I'm not scrapping my old behavior modification methods, but now I see them as only part of the total package.

•◆•

When Is Medication Needed?

Only a doctor or psychiatrist can determine when medication is appropriate treatment for a particular case of ADD. In moderate or severe cases, we recommend medication management as *part of a multimodal treatment approach,* including education, counseling, behavior management, and group support. (If you have a history of substance abuse—including alcohol—be sure your doctor or psychiatrist knows that before prescribing medication.)

However, the use of medication management *alone* in the treatment of adult ADD is not recommended. Medication will not solve all the problems of the ADDer, but it will (probably) give the ADDer solid footing on which to approach his or her problems.

Medication is not necessary for all adults with ADD. In mild cases of ADD, a client may do well unmedicated. At times, merely the knowledge that a person's symptoms are caused by ADD, not by a lack of intelligence or motivation, is enough to encourage him or her to develop realistic expectations and creative coping skills. The knowledge itself can break the downward spiral of poor performance and poor self-esteem.

142

"Now that I know I have an actual disorder," one ADD client said, "I can work on rebuilding my self-esteem. I can channel my energies in new ways. I can surround myself with others to pick up and run with my ideas. As long as my problem was invisible, it was impossible to fight back. At least now I know the face of the dragon I am fighting."

What Medications Are Available?

The medications currently being prescribed for ADD generally fall into one of the following classifications:

- Psychostimulants
- Tricyclic antidepressants
- Selective Serotonin-Reuptake Inhibitors (SSRIs)
- Miscellaneous drugs

The exact mechanism is not yet clear, but it is believed that the anti-ADD effects of these various medications are due to changes they produce in the amounts of chemical messengers transmitted between neurons in the brain. These are called neurotransmitters. The primary mechanisms are thought to be due to dopamine and norepinephrine amounts. Although the classifications of medication affects the brain differently, they seem to be helpful in treating adult ADD. Let's look at them in more detail.

PSYCHOSTIMULANTS

The most commonly presecribed group of medications for the treatment of adult ADD are the psychostimulants. It is estimated that approximately

143

70 to 80 percent of children with ADD have shown improvement with the use of psychostimulants. While estimates are not yet available for adults, many clients report significant improvement with the use of these drugs. Common medications in this classification include:

- Ritalin
- Dexedrine
- Cylert
- Desoxyn
- Adderall

TRICYCLIC ANTIDEPRESSANTS

Psychostimulants in general tend to be superior in the treatment of ADD, but many ADDers do not respond to them or have difficulty with their side effects. Some of these people have the best results with a tricyclic antidepressant. This classification of medications is often recommended when the ADDer also has depression, anxiety, or an obsessive-compulsive disorder that needs to be treated along with the ADD.

Common medications in this category include:

- Desipramine
- Imipramine
- Anafranil
- Amitriptylin

SELECTIVE SEROTONIN RE-UPTAKE INHIBITORS

Occasionally clinicians report benefit with the use of medications that increase the levels of serotonin transmitted in the brain. But most of the more successful treatments for pure ADD affect dopamine and norepinephrine levels between nerve endings. These medications are usually combined with psychostimulants or recommended when depression needs to be treated along with ADD.

Common medications in this classification include:

- Prozac
- Zoloft
- Paxil
- Luvox

MISCELLANEOUS DRUGS

Other medications that have been tried with some frequency in the treatment of adult ADD include:

- Nortriptyline
- Wellbutrin
- Effexor
- Clonidine

In addition, there are nearly thirty other medications that are also being prescribed less frequently to help those with ADD, and other medications are currently being used outside the U.S.

It is important for an ADDer to realize that there are numerous options for medical management, including the classification from which a medication is chosen, the specific drug chosen from the classification, the possible combination of medications, and the dosage and frequency of the medication taken. If you do not get good results from your first trial of medication, don't give up! Take the time to communicate with your doctor and work together to review other options. Some ADDers have needed to try three or four different medications in order to find the one that managed their symptoms most effectively.

Resistance to Medication

WHICH IS THE REAL ME?

"I don't want to change who I am."

"If I get rid of the ADD symptoms, will there be anything left of me?"

"Who am I without ADD?"

We have heard all of these comments many times over. People are often wary of beginning medication, even for something as serious as ADD, because they fear they will lose something of themselves.

For many adults with ADD, their identity is closely linked with their disorder. The ADDer has spent a lifetime coping with the symptoms — the forgetfulness, the difficulties attending to tasks, impulsivity, etc. The symptoms of ADD have become fused with their perception of who they are. Their sense of self-worth has been dramatically assaulted on a regular basis due to these symptoms. But in some cases they have built a sense of uniqueness on these very symptoms. They become "Disorganized Dan" or "Sorry-I'm-Late Sally." They learn to accept these qualities in themselves, and the people around them expect these ADDers to be a certain way. Furthermore, they have made lifestyle and career choices based on these ADD characteristics.

146

It is no wonder that some people are hesitant to amputate these familiar aspects of themselves through medication management.

Individual counseling is essential in sorting through these identity issues and helping to evaluate the risks and possible benefits of medication management. If a client does choose to take medication, counseling is still necessary to help with this "identity change."

WHO'S IN CONTROL?

"If I succeed at my job by taking medication, is it really me who's succeeding, or the drugs?" This is another point of resistance to ADD medication.

We've told you about Laura, whose school grades changed so abruptly after she began medication that her teacher accused her of cheating. But some clients have that same view of their own achievements under medication. Somehow, they think, it's "cheating," because the drug is doing their work for them. They don't take credit for the things they accomplish while medicated. The medication may be doing a great job at work, at school, in the home, or wherever, but the client sees himself as "still the same old failure."

Counseling is generally very helpful in sorting out such issues regarding identity and self-esteem. It's important to see what the medication does. The medication itself does not create any new ideas, it merely releases the ideas already in the client's mind. It's like clearing a logjam: the medication does not make new logs; it just orders the flow so the logs float downstream.

The ADDer on medication is still the same person. It's just that his or her brain is put in better working order. In a way, medication helps ADDers to be themselves; it's the ADD that has restricted their self-expression.

If you hire a maid to clean your house, does the house now belong to the maid? No, of course not. It's still your house, and its new, clean condition should enable you to enjoy it more, and perhaps even entertain guests. In the same way, medication sort of "cleans your house," allowing you to enjoy your own thinking and present it to others.

Still, some clients feel that they are more in control if they take medication only on an as-needed basis, and not all the time. Some types of ADD medication can be used in this manner. (This approach also reduces the amount of medication that is consumed.)

One client, an architect, found that he was better able to design buildings while not on the medication. Somehow the imagination he needed to dream up new architectural possibilities was diminished by his medication. He decided not to take the medication when he needed to work on creative projects, but to take it when he needed to follow up on details.

If your physician allows, and if you decide to take your medication "as needed," be sure to get input from your significant others about when it's needed. We knew one ADD client who decided to take medication to get him through his working day, but then go off the medication while he relaxed at home at night. His wife, however, was not as keen on that arrangement. She felt that there was no point in trying to talk with him and express her views while he was unable to focus and concentrate. On nights when she had important things to talk about, she insisted that he take his medication at home, too.

You might consider it something like wearing glasses. After a long day at work, would you stop wearing your glasses for a while? If you had minimal vision difficulties, you might answer yes. And some clients with minimal ADD may also choose not to take medication during more relaxed, less structured times. If you are severely nearsighted, however, it would be ridiculous to set aside your glasses for any length of time—especially if you had to do anything important. The same is probably true of severe ADD.

Some experts recommend taking occasional "drug holidays"—going off the medication for a day, or a weekend, or a week. This can sometimes help a client (and a counselor) to assess the progress that has been made and the skills that have been acquired. Perhaps the medication is no longer needed. A "drug holiday" may also minimize the potential side effects of the medication. It may also confirm the need for medication and help everyone involved to be sure of the course chosen for treatment.

The key thing to remember about medication management is that you are managing your medication; the medication is not managing you. You are giving it permission to help you focus on important tasks. You may choose to take a lot or a little. You may choose to take it all the time or only once in a while. But you are choosing. You are in control.

How Can You Tell If It Works?

My (Michele's) father also has ADD. At first he was reluctant to try medication, but he eventually changed his mind. Once he tried the medication, he reported being able to focus for longer periods of time while he worked on his computer. He also took the medication before attending a meeting, and noticed that he was able to remember some of what was said.

Over time, however, he became convinced that the medication really didn't do much for him anymore. He would stop taking it for a while. I saw him on several occasions when he was off the medication and I could tell the difference within the first three minutes or so. This amazed my father. As far as he was concerned, the medication had stopped working, it was having no effect. But I could see almost immediately that he had not taken it.

When he attempted to help fix something at our house when he was on the medication, he would fix the item with minimal fuss. While not on the medication, a simple task would become an all-day project, tools would be broken or misplaced, additional parts would become broken, and directions could not be followed.

At a restaurant, while off medication, he would spill the water, drop food, knock over various items and go off on tangents during con-versations. While on medication, he was able to focus in our bridge group well enough to earn the high score of the night, not spill anything and follow along with the conversations.

While not on the medication, he would simply load, unload, and transfer programs on his computer. While on medication, he was able to create a flyer and develop a mailing list. The difference was very clear to me, though he missed it.

•◆•

It is sometimes very difficult for those with ADD to evaluate the effectiveness of medications objectively. Research indicates that the report of someone close to the client may be more reliable than a self-report. Maybe, over time, the ADDer on medication forgets what it was like to be unfocused and, because he or she is now focusing regularly, fails to see any more day-to-day improvement. Thus the ADDer concludes that the medication is less effective, when a spouse or family member can easily see the change.

There is clearly a need for some form of objective as well as subjective monitoring of the effectiveness of medication. Self-reports can also be distorted by a few remaining symptoms that may not be caused by the ADD. The client might think, "I'm still having problems, therefore the medication isn't working," when the medication is working, and it's isolating those non-ADD problems that still need to be dealt with.

We have found it helpful to have both the client and a close observer (perhaps a spouse) complete a rating scale on a regular basis to help add objectivity to the medication management process. It also helps us determine what is not being taken care of by the medication and may need to be addressed through further medical intervention, assessment or counseling.

In some cases, of course, people are clearly able to notice the differences in their lives in terms of achievement, interpersonal relationships, organization, and dreams. It should be noted, however, that medication seems to work only in about 70 percent of ADD cases. So a doctor or counselor should monitor its effects closely.

Making Informed Choices

A client needs to make an informed choice regarding medical management. This requires information gathering—a key component of ADD treatment. There are various treatment options, and these are each promoted by various professionals in the field. If you are considering treatment for ADD, you need to learn about these methods.

Some doctors and counselors recommend only medication management, while others will only recommend counseling. Among those who recommend medication, some suggest constant use while others say clients should use medication sparingly, only when needed for special events. Some will recommend that you take the least amount possible to get some relief from symptoms, whereas others will recommend that you continue to increase the medication until you reach maximum benefit.

Beware of the personal bias of the professional with whom you are working. As a psychologist who once was strongly against medication management but now favors it, I (Michele) am very aware of the weight my bias brings into a session. I try to present all the currently known treatment options in an objective manner. I generally encourage clients to seek out a second opinion from someone who is less enthusiastic regarding medical management as a piece of the treatment plan, in order to have a more balanced perspective.

However, not all professionals are as up front about their personal biases. This can have a profound impact on a client's decision-making process.

As with any physical problem, you should never be shy about seeking a second opinion. No responsible doctor or counselor would object to that. In addition, review the literature available concerning ADD. There are several other fine books available that include informative chapters on medication management.[1] ADD support groups are also a good resource for helping you make intelligent treatment choices.

All medications have side effects. These need to be carefully evaluated in order to assess whether the potential benefit is worth the possible risk. Please check with your health care provider for complete information regarding possible risks for any medication you are considering.

Do your homework, consult well-trained professionals, and make informed choices about treatment. You may have a great deal to gain.

JUST THE FACTS

- There are numerous options to consider regarding the medical management of ADD. Four classifications of effective ADD medication are available, with several specific drug options within each category.

- In severe and moderate cases of ADD, medication is recommended as part of a treatment plan that includes education, counseling, behavior modification, and support groups. Those with mild ADD may also benefit from medication. Consult your doctor.

- Some people resist taking medication because they fear the loss of key aspects of their identity. This underscores the need for counseling along with medication.

(continued)

- Some resist medication because they fear loss of control. But there are various ways to use the medication, and the client does stay in control.

- Sometimes people don't know whether their medication is working. But the people around them can usually tell.

- A person considering medication for ADD needs to make an informed choice rather than a merely emotional one.

- Choose the members of your treatment team carefully. All professionals are not equally educated or skilled in treating adults with ADD. Don't be afraid to seek a second opinion.

NOTE

1. Other books you might want to review for the information they provide on medication management include: Edward M. Hallowell, M.D., and John J. Ratey, M.D., *Driven to Distraction* (New York: Pantheon Books, 1994); Kate Kelly and Peggy Ramundo, *So You Mean I'm Not Lazy, Stupid or Crazy?* (Cincinnati, OH: Tyrell and Jerem Press, 1993); Paul H. Wender, M.D., *The Hyperactive Child, Adolescent, and Adult* (New York: Oxford University Press, 1987); and Russell A. Barkley, Ph.D., *Attention-Deficit Hyperactivity Disorder: A Handbook for Diagnosis and Treatment* (New York: The Guilford Press, 1990).

CHAPTER ELEVEN

COUNSELING

THE TENTACLES OF ADD reach far into the lives of those who have the disorder. ADD affects your self-esteem, your ability to learn, your career, and your relationships, often wreaking havoc in various forms and to varying degrees. Once ADD is diagnosed and treatment is begun, those residual effects of ADD still must be addressed.

Out of necessity, ADDers learn many *coping skills*. These may be rather ingenious as the person grows up with ADD, but once the ADD tendencies are being managed through medication or other means, the coping strategies may actually interfere with the ADDer's progress.

For example, many ADDers develop an "uh-huh" habit in conversation. They may have tuned out the speaker, but they don't want to be embarrassed, so they mutter "uh-huh" to indicate that they're listening and that they understand. This is a hard habit to break. Even when an ADDer, under treatment, *is* following a conversation, he or she may continue the "uh-huh" habit and never ask for clarification of an obscure point. ADDers become so good at fake listening that it's hard to listen for real.

Other skills necessary for normal adult life may have been missed during the ADD "blinks." These include *social skills* as well as *academic skills.* Ordinary perceptions, which most people pick up naturally as they grow, may have to be intentionally learned by the adult ADDer who is seeking treatment for the first time.

One client was thrilled the first time he saw his wife get angry. "I always got angry so quick and exploded, I never really noticed her," he explained. "We were having a heated discussion and I noticed her face getting red. I said, 'Hey, you're starting to get angry, aren't you?' It was interesting to watch her. Then she raised her voice and clenched her fist. I watched her in amazement because I had never noticed this before. I commented again on her anger and she got mad and left the room because I wasn't focused on the issue, but I was excited because it was the first time in my life that I had actually seen her get mad before I exploded myself." Now, being treated for ADD, he was seeing some social nuances he had missed before, like his wife's display of anger.

• ◆ •

This is common. ADDers in treatment are often seeing and hearing new things—the tones of voice that mean "No" even though the person is saying "Yes"; or the subtle cues given when you have over-stayed your welcome and it is time to leave. Many counseling sessions are spent interpreting events that have taken place during the week and reframing or clarifying them. In some counseling offices, ADDers even take time to practice new social skills.

ADD also teaches a *learned helplessness* and a *poor self-esteem*. "There is no sense in trying because I've already tried this a million times before and failed. I'm not going to keep banging my head into a brick wall." Outside encouragement is very helpful in encouraging an ADDer to try again or to try in a different way. Counselors need to work at developing an ADDer's view of self. Some clients are rebuilding a whole new sense of identity.

In addition, there are many *family and personal issues* that require counseling. Some of these have been caused or made worse by the ADD. In other cases, the issues may be independent of ADD, but ADD has kept the person (or family) from dealing with them. As an ADDer begins treatment, many of these old issues emerge and demand attention. For the first time, the ADDer is able to give them the attention they need.

The Five Stages in Individual Therapy

We find five distinct stages in the counseling process: The "Aha, I have it!" stage, followed by grief, support, exploration, and dreams.

INDIVIDUAL THERAPY
The Five Stages

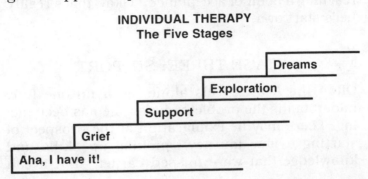

Dreams

Exploration

Support

Grief

Aha, I have it!

STAGE ONE: AHA, I HAVE IT!

In the first stage, the counselor needs to help you deal with the feelings the diagnosis has aroused—from despair to joy to everything in between. Some ADDers are elated with the diagnosis; suddenly they have a reason for the difficulties they have faced all their lives. Others become anxious or worried with this new label. Frequently they feel a great deal of confusion, a feeling of being overloaded and overwhelmed with this new information and its ramifications.

STAGE TWO: GRIEF

We grieve over losses in our lives, and the newly diagnosed ADDer usually is facing up to some past losses for the first time. Often the ADDer feels regret about missed opportunities, broken relationships, and misunderstandings. "If only I had known about this before, maybe I wouldn't have gotten divorced, maybe I would have been able to finish college, maybe. . . ."

Grief is something you go through; you can't take a shortcut. A counselor's job is to aid you in a steady progression through the grief, finally reaching a point of acceptance. "Okay, that's reality. Let's start over."

STAGE THREE: SUPPORT

Often the ADDer feels alone, as if no one fully understands the problems he or she has been facing. There may be exhilaration at the prospect of starting a new journey—picking up skills and knowledge that were missed earlier—but it can also be scary. At this stage, the counselor provides encouragement and advice.

Identity and self-esteem issues can be tackled now in more depth. The ADDer needs to develop the confidence that he or she can be a consistently valuable, productive member of society.

People with ADD need help to see the positive aspects of the disorder they struggle with. Most notably, ADDers generally have the ability to think "outside the box," to think of things in new ways. They frequently pull in ideas from a variety of sources. In an age of specialization, this is a valuable commodity. ADDers tend to be very real, open and honest, not superficial. They are often able to "see through" phony people and empathize with other wounded souls. These are all good qualities that an ADDer can enjoy and, in a sense, be proud of.

At this point in the counseling process, therapy groups are extremely helpful. (See section on group therapy, beginning on page 160.)

STAGE FOUR: EXPLORATION

In some ways, you might say the ADDer in treatment is learning how to live. He or she is exchanging old coping skills for healthier new habits. The ADDer gains information he missed the first time around and acquires new life skills.

This is an exciting stage of counseling. A host of old problems are addressed and new alternatives explored. It doesn't have to be the same old story over and over again. You can try things a different way now that you have an explanation for your behavior.

STAGE FIVE: DREAMS

What would you like to do now? If the exploration stage was exciting, the fifth stage is positively inspiring. The ADDer needs hope to move forward on his or her own, propelled by dreams of a satisfying future.

One woman in one of our ADD support groups was fifty-two years old and had hit a "glass ceiling" in her job. She was never considered for an administrative position due to her inability to organize material. But once she was diagnosed with ADD and began treatment, a world of opportunities opened to her. By the time the support group stopped meeting, she was considering taking a new job as a company's national director!

•◆•

It's never too late to start dreaming. What are your dreams?

Group Therapy

At a certain time in the counseling process, a therapist may suggest that a client join a therapy group. It can be highly therapeutic to share one's problems and progress with others who are in the same boat.

We should make a technical distinction between an ADD therapy group and an ADD support group. An ADD support group is often organized and led by persons with ADD who generally don't have a professional counseling background. Generally, the purpose is to share information rather than to work on individual issues. An ADD therapy group is organized and led by a professional counselor with experience in ADD and in group therapy. The purpose of the therapy group is to provide information and to work on the individual ADD-related issues each member is struggling with.

Therapy groups are generally time-limited— ours are six to ten sessions. The groups meet for one-and-a-half hours each week. We spend half of each group session in a structured educational talk and the other half in open discussion.

ADD therapy groups are a powerful tool for healing the wounds of ADD. The struggle with ADD is often an individual, silent struggle. It is immensely encouraging to know there are others like you. You are not alone.

WHAT TO EXPECT IN GROUP THERAPY

At the first meeting of an ADD therapy group, everyone seems apprehensive. Who will be there? What will they look like? I know that I'm not the only one who has made such a mess of my life, but will these other people understand me or judge me?

An ADD group is usually a diverse group. I'm always taken aback by the different forms and faces of ADD. In one group we had three with hyperactivity and three without hyperactivity. It was hard to believe they all suffered from the same disorder until they began to share their stories. The common thread became clear as the stories unfolded.

In our groups, we make a point of generating a list of positive characteristics of ADD. We are well aware of ADD's difficulties, but few ADDers have thought much about its positive components. This process always becomes a highlight of the group process as members begin to see positive characteristics in themselves.

We also have lively discussions regarding treatment options for managing ADD. Almost every group has some discussion regarding the use of medication. Another common topic is alternative strategies for managing ADD.

"The group was a most valuable piece of putting my life back together," said one of our group members.

"It was good to hear other people talk about how it is for them," said another, "because it was reassuring to know I'm not the only one. I'm not losing my mind."

Yet another said, "I have gained a much better understanding of myself and how ADD has affected my life. The group has also helped to build my self-confidence and determination in dealing with and overcoming my negative ADD ways. It has been great to be able to relate to such a wonderful group of people."

If you can find an ADD therapy group in your area, we urge you to give it a try.

JUST THE FACTS

Counseling is a necessary component of ADD treatment because of:

- Previous coping skills that now hinder growth

- Missed social and academic skills that need to be learned

- Learned helplessness and low self-esteem

- Other personal and family issues that arise after an ADD diagnosis.

The ADD counseling process consists of five stages:

1. Aha, I have it!

2. Grief

3. Support

4. Exploration

5. Dreams

Group therapy is extremely helpful as adults with ADD compare notes, positive and negative, with each other.

CHAPTER TWELVE

BEHAVIOR MODIFICATION

MARK WAS GREATLY hampered by his ADD, but was adamantly opposed to taking any kind of medication. He grew up with a drug-addicted father and an alcoholic mother, so he feared exposing himself to anything that might become habitual. Even though his doctor tried to assure him that medication should be safe, as long as he used it properly, he still would not consider this leading treatment.

•◆•

If you have personal or family addictions in your background, taking stimulants may create some concern. Some doctors will recommend that you use medication other than stimulants, or no medication at all. Other professionals will tell you that as long as you don't abuse the dosage, Ritalin and other stimulants are relatively safe.

If you have addictive tendences, we urge caution and recommend that the prescribing physician be fully informed of your background as part of the evaluation process.

REASONS PEOPLE GIVE FOR NOT TAKING MEDICATION

1. "I have addictions in my background."

2. "I'm opposed to any kind of medication."

3. "My ADD symptoms are manageable without it."

4. "I've tried it and it doesn't work for me."

What should you do if you do not want to take medication? Or if the medical alternatives seem too drastic to you? There are behavioral treatment options for you that will not change your brain chemistry nor the way you think, but can help to alleviate some of the most negative characteristics of the disorder.

⬩◆⬩

Mark needed help adjusting his schedule and organizing his life. He worked as a salesman in an office, mostly doing phone solicitations. He was very good with people and did well on the phone. He could build relationships with new clients and turn them into steady customers. But as you might guess, paperwork was his downfall. He would usually fall well behind in turning in his sales reports, and his financial figures were often wrong. The more he struggled, the more he avoided dealing with it, and the further behind he became.

Things got so bad that Mark sought help in order to save his job. Through counseling, Mark reordered his life. He set up a weekly routine in which every Wednesday and Friday he stayed off

166

the phones completely. On those days, he shut his office door, had all his calls held, and focused on writing up the orders from the previous day or two. He used a calculator for his figures and checked his work twice. His clients learned to reach him on Monday, Tuesday, or Thursday, and Mark learned to stay current on all his work. He also spent Friday afternoon cleaning off his desk and organizing his files.

The result was not increased sales, yet Mark was able to maintain his income level while feeling much better about himself and his job. Life became manageable! Mark learned that he needed to keep a routine that forced him to stay organized and focused.

•◆•

Most ADDers need some sort of lifestyle or behavioral change in order to manage their lives better — *even if they are on medication.* There are several simple tools that can make life much more productive and fulfilling.

Behavioral Techniques

ADD affects different people in different ways. As you seek behavioral ways to cope with ADD, you first need to figure out which behaviors you want to cope with.

If you had a complete interview for ADD with a psychologist or counselor, you may have filled out a "problem checklist" of some type. That gives you a place to start. You can use this to isolate the areas of your life that are most affected by ADD, and it can give you an agenda to begin your behavior modification.

We recommend you work through these behavioral

issues with a professional counselor. That will give you the one-on-one observation and accountability you need. However, the "problem checklist" below may give you a running start on some of the issues you're dealing with.

PROBLEM CHECKLIST
Check all that apply to you.
☐ **1.** I need to learn more about ADD.
☐ **2.** I do things impulsively, sometimes crazy or even dangerous things.
☐ **3.** I am always on the go; I need to slow down.
☐ **4.** I don't know how to handle my emotions and frustrations.
☐ **5.** I need to build my self-image.
☐ **6.** I find it hard to control my temper.
☐ **7.** I need to overcome a substance abuse issue.
☐ **8.** I need help in organizing or scheduling my life.
☐ **9.** I have a hard time putting my tasks in order and doing the most important things first.
☐ **10.** I need help organizing and handling my finances.
☐ **11.** I start things but don't finish them.
☐ **12.** I need help planning my day and following through on that plan.
(continued)

☐ **13.** I forget things too often.

☐ **14.** As a student, I am having difficulty keeping up with my classes.

☐ **15.** I don't communicate well with others.

☐ **16.** I should be a better listener.

☐ **17.** My closest relationships are in trouble.

☐ **18.** I need a quiet place to work.

☐ **19.** At work, I have difficulty focusing on one thing at a time.

☐ **20.** I don't think I've found the right job for me yet.

Go back over the things you have checked and choose three that stand out as your worst problem areas. Circle these.

Then get a different colored pen or pencil and go through it again with a spouse, family member, or close friend. What does that person see as your greatest challenges? Circle the top two or three mentioned by this person.

Now, from the issues circled, choose the three you need to work on the most. List them here.

_____

_____

_____

Now go to the "key" (follows) for these particular problem areas to see how you might begin to address them.

PROBLEM AREA 1: EDUCATION

Education is a powerful tool in coping with ADD. It can minimize frustration, build self-confidence, and help a person choose wise strategies for living.

You have already started the education process by reading this book. Your next step should be to call a local CHADD organization (Children with Attention Deficit Disorders). Don't let the word Children fool you. Just like the diagnosis itself, CHADD started out by focusing on kids (and educating their parents about ADD). But as adult ADD became more prevalent, CHADD expanded its outreach to include adults as well.

CHADD's resources include books, tapes, videos, and a list of support groups available around the country. Call (305)587-3700 to reach their national headquarters.

There is also an ADD Warehouse catalog that lists available books, tapes, and videos. Call (800)233-9273 to receive this free catalog of products.

Since research is constantly being done on ADD, and scientists are learning more about the disorder, be alert to breaking stories in the media about new discoveries. Every year or so you might scan a library's database (or the Internet) for new articles on ADD.

PROBLEM AREA 2: IMPULSIVITY

Impulsivity is a major symptom of ADD. It may manifest itself in relatively minor ways or in potentially devastating ways.

Review chapter 7, on impulsivity, especially the suggestions on pages 105-106.

PROBLEM AREA 3: HYPERACTIVITY

Hyperactivity is another major symptom of ADD. It is seen mostly in children, but many adults display hyperactive behavior, even though it may be somewhat muted.

Review chapter 8, on hyperactivity, especially the suggestions on page 116.

PROBLEM AREAS 4–7:
COUNSELING ISSUES

Many issues of identity and emotions are raised by ADD. This is why counseling is an essential part of the treatment process — not only to learn new ways to *act* but also to learn new ways to *think* and *feel* about yourself, about others, and about ADD.

Review chapter 11, on counseling, especially the suggestions on pages 157-160.

PROBLEM AREAS 8–12:
ORGANIZATION

High school or college students sometimes take extra courses in study skills to help them manage their schoolwork. Adults with ADD usually need something similar—some training in "life skills" — to help them manage their lives.

See chapter 13, on organization, especially the suggestions on The Three S's summarized at the end of the chapter.

PROBLEM AREAS 13–14: LEARNING

Learning problems affect adults with ADD as well as children, although they are most obvious in organized classroom situations. College students with ADD often have trouble keeping up with course work because of the inconsistency of their attention. Once they fall behind, it's hard to catch up. Many ADDers keep fighting this battle as they enroll in adult education courses to make up for what they missed in college.

But even those who don't take classes can experience "learning disability" in the forgetfulness of daily life. If your spouse tells you to get five things at the store and you only remember two, that can be a problem.

See chapter 14, on learning, taking special note of the suggestions on pages 207-208.

PROBLEM AREAS 15–17: RELATIONSHIPS

For many ADDers, the most painful part of their disorder is the havoc it plays in their relationships. Marriages have broken up due to ADD. Some ADDers have been alienated from their parents or siblings or closest friends.

Communication is crucial to any relationship, and ADDers need to pay special attention to this (which isn't easy!). You must own up to your problem and ask your loved ones to understand and be part of the solutions you're seeking.

We deal with communication and other issues in chapter 15, on relationships. Take special note of the suggestions on pages 223-227.

PROBLEM AREAS 18–20: WORK

ADDers often have difficulty finding the right job, doing all the necessary aspects of a job, or getting along with coworkers. Often there are problems with the work*place*—it's too noisy or too distracting.

If this is a problem area for you, be sure to read chapter 16, on work-related issues, taking special note of the suggestions on pages 242-245.

JUST THE FACTS

For several reasons, some people with ADD prefer to use behavioral treatment options alone, instead of medication. Even in cases where medication is used, however, behavioral changes are essential for the proper treatment of ADD.

Adults with ADD tend to have unique challenges in the following areas:

● Education

● Impulsivity

● Hyperactivity

● Identity and emotions

● Organization

● Learning

● Relationships

● Work

This chapter points you in the right direction for addressing each of these problem areas.

173

PART FIVE

OVERCOMING ADD DIFFICULTIES

CHAPTER THIRTEEN

ORGANIZATION

JANE'S* HOUSE WAS SO disorganized that she had stuff literally stacked thigh-high in several rooms. Walking through her bedroom was like parting the Red Sea — there was only a narrow path in which to walk and a small section of her bed on which to lie. Her son confirmed this. They both watched a video about adult ADD, which included scenes of a disorganized, messy home.

"That's nothing," Jane's son said. "Look, you can still see the floor, and those stacks of stuff are only a foot high!"

•◆•

Of course, Jane is an extreme example of a disorganized ADD sufferer. But many ADDers tell tales of lost papers, forgotten meetings, and frustrated spouses and coworkers. Disorganization is a prime side-effect of the distractibility of ADDers. With ADD, people start projects and get sidetracked: They begin to straighten up and are distracted by the first thing they pick up, they drop what they're doing to do something else, and then they can't remember where they dropped the first thing.

Bill* is an incredibly creative architect with what I would call "moderate" organizational difficulties. He would imagine and design wonderfully innovative office buildings and stores, but he could not organize himself enough to follow through with the details of putting the designs on paper. His missed deadlines were hurting an otherwise brilliant career.

There are also many ADDers with only "mild" organizational problems. They tend to function all right, but usually with a great deal of stress or anxiety. They are frequently late for appointments, and often misplace important papers (though they usually find these after some searching). Their disorganization is a source of stress for them and an annoyance for others.

Knowing Versus Doing

With ADD it is not a lack of knowing what to do that causes the difficulties with organization. It is the inability to do what they know they should and could do. That is part of the frustration of this disorder.

A person with ADD in the mild or moderate range may even improve his or her organizational skills in a particular area of life for a period of time if highly motivated to do so. But can this person *sustain* these organizational skills? This is where ADD adults fail. They know what they want to do. They may even be able to do it for a short period of time. For some reason they stop. Now they feel like failures. They are generally viewed by others as lazy, unmotivated, or rebellious because they have already demonstrated that they can be better organized, therefore they must not be trying. Most people tolerate those who have an *inability* to perform at a certain level, but most people get very annoyed with someone who has shown the ability to perform at a certain level on one day and is not performing at the same level the next day.

The inconsistency of organization in the lives of many ADDers leads to poor self-esteem. They don't understand their own failings.

INCONSISTENCY

This inconsistency puzzles the researchers as well. How can a person's behavior be fine one day and erratic the next?

Dr. Russell A. Barkley, one of the leading ADD scholars, notes, "What is not so clear from research is whether this deficit in paying attention reflects a primary deficit in *sustained* attention or is secondary to the problem of *behavioral disinhibition*." In other words, does the ADDer's ability to pay attention just "wear out" after a while, or does the ADDer lose the ability to say no to distractions? Barkley goes on to support the latter view, that it is *behavioral disinhibition* that creates problems for those with ADD. This is described as a proneness to become easily led away from the task at hand, and not being able to stop oneself from doing "more interesting" activities.

"The most consistent findings," Barkley says, "are for a primary deficit in behavioral or response inhibition, the ability to delay responses, or the tolerance for delay intervals within the tasks. Thus, the primary component of ADHD is more one of disinhibition or poor delay of responding than inattention."[1]

So the problem is not that the ADDer can't

179

attend to things, but that the ADDer attends to *everything!* If the current task stops being interesting, if it does not reward the ADDer's attention any longer, then the ADDer's mind flits off to something else that promises a greater reward.

Another noted ADD expert, Dr. Thomas E. Brown, comes at the problem a different way. He refers to the definition of ADD (ADHD) in *DSM IV,* the psychologist's diagnostic manual. One criterion is: "appears apathetic or unmotivated." That item, says Brown, "is the tip of a massive iceberg. What looks like apathy or lack of motivation is a chronic problem with *activation*, which we believe is central to understanding ADD/WO (ADD without hyperactivity).

"Many of those with ADD/WO report chronic problems with 'getting cranked up' to do tasks, even tasks they recognize as urgent and important for their own welfare. . . . Often this activation problem in ADD/WO extends to sustaining energy for tasks. Many of those we see report great difficulty in keeping up their energy to read or write or do another task."[2]

As we said earlier, it is *expensive* for the ADDer to pay attention. It takes great effort to focus on a particular task, and it takes great effort to sustain that focus. There is a limit to the effort an ADDer can apply to a task before his or her energy is "spent." This may be the key to the inconsistency of ADDers' attention.

Let's say you worked at a rather sedentary job, but suddenly were asked to unload a truck full of heavy crates. No one would blame you for taking it easy the rest of the day. You're tired! You have expended a lot of energy.

Similarly, the ADDer may work hard one day

to stay "on task," maintaining concentration to get a job done, but that's hard work. The next day, the person may take it easy, may stop working so hard, and may let his or her mind go wherever it wants. Barkley would say the person lacks the energy to screen out distractions (disinhibition), while Brown would say the person lacks the energy to focus on a new task (activation).

The Keys to Improvement

Many adults with ADD have shelves full of how-to-organize-your-life books. Some buy them for themselves (often as New Year's resolutions), and some receive them as gifts from well-intentioned spouses, friends, or coworkers. Unfortunately, ADDers are frequently unable to focus long enough to read them or they often forget what they have read or they start to implement the ideas with all the best intentions but fail to follow through.

No one is more troubled by these tendencies than the ADDers themselves. They feel that they are fighting a losing battle.

For that reason, the first key to improving organizational skills is *hope*. The second is *understanding*. First, the person with ADD needs to believe that his or her life can become more organized — and this is tough after repeated attempts and failures. Second, the person must understand the nature of ADD and must set reasonable goals at a reasonable pace.

We love the title of a book on ADD: *You Mean I'm Not Lazy, Stupid Or Crazy?*[3] After a lifetime of accepting those labels, an ADDer must accept himself or herself as a person with a disorder — but not with a moral shortcoming. That disorder can be managed. Although it won't be easy, you *can* take small steps to improve the organization of your life and lessen the negative effects of seemingly inevitable disorganization.

Once an ADDer understands the reason for his or her difficulties, and has hope that things can change, he can have renewed energy to tackle the problem.

The Role of Medication

One of the most obvious ways for an ADDer to improve organizational skills is to take medication. We have seen dramatic changes in the organizational abilities of many adults with ADD once they went on medication. We've seen notable improvement especially in those with moderate to severe levels of ADD.

Amazingly, it seems that some ADDers don't even recognize their own disorganization. They become so familiar with the stacks of paper and piles of stuff that they stop paying attention to them. Medication can often improve their focus to the point that they *notice* the surrounding disarray. One client explained, "It wasn't until I took medication that I even saw the mess. My desk was always piled high with papers, and I almost never got my work in on time. That was just normal for me. Once I started medication, I not only saw the mess, but I had the energy and ability to focus on the problem. My desk is clean!"

One friend proudly showed me his desk after he had begun taking medication for ADD. It was covered with "only" about two inches of papers. There were papers sticking out of half-open drawers. "At least now I see them!" he exclaimed. "I never even noticed all these papers before!"

The medication had not turned this man into

a neat freak. Far from it! But it was giving him the initial focus he needed. Now he could learn how to keep those piles of papers from accumulating.

Despite such glowing testimonials, we must be clear on several points:

Medication does not solve all the problems. ADDers learn bad habits as they live with their disorder. Many have never learned basic organizational strategies because they could never succeed at applying them. Medication can improve one's ability to focus, to screen out distractions, but the ADDer must still learn how to organize his or her life. That's why counseling and working on organizational strategies play a crucial role in the management of ADD.

Medication does not work for everybody. Studies show that 70 to 80 percent of ADD clients show some improvement under medication, but that leaves 20 to 30 percent who don't.

Some improvement may be seen without medication. For those with ADD who don't want to take medication, they can also make some progress by working hard to adopt some of the organizational strategies mentioned below. Depending on the level of one's ADD, it will be a tough fight. But some improvements are possible.

The Three S's

Organizational management for ADDers breaks into three categories: Self, Space, and Stuff.

SELF

Keeping oneself organized is the ultimate challenge for those with ADD. You might think the very fact that a person has ADD makes self-organization impossible. But it can be done. In fact, some ADDers have coped with this disorder by becoming *extremely* organized. By relying on the routine of organization, they have become able to manage their lives effectively.

1. Structure. Many find a highly structured environment conducive to getting things done. With an absence of such structure, many get easily distracted by the multiple options available and get nothing important accomplished.

One client, for example, always pays bills on Friday, does the laundry on Monday, and goes grocery shopping on Tuesday. She follows this pattern religiously. If the grocery store were ever closed on Tuesday, she would be thrown off. She feels that if she adjusts her schedule she would be too distracted to get her tasks completed.

2. Priorities. Establishing priorities is extremely important. Unfortunately, those with ADD find this very difficult to do. Earlier we mentioned the inability to "weigh" things in the mind. For the ADDer, many items seem to entertain the brain as equally attractive options. In the midst of trying to write a term paper for college or finish a business report, a phone call to a friend may claim equal importance.

It is helpful to keep in mind the slogan "First things first," also the title of a recent book by Stephen Covey. The ADDer will not *naturally* rate things according to priority. The ADD brain does not know what "first things" to put first. But the ADDer can establish a habit of *intentionally* rating the priority of tasks. Maybe it becomes a routine at the beginning of the day; you make a list and select the three most important tasks in order. Then make it a point to put first things first. (It may be helpful to ask others for input as you begin to learn to prioritize.)

3. Small steps. Although many ADD sufferers have read about, heard lectures about, or attended workshops on time management, many fail to put the recommendations into action. Often they put down the book or come home from the workshop and determine to change their lives radically. Everything must go! Old habits will be swept out and new habits adopted.

How long does that determination last? A day? A week? These people soon become frustrated because they are trying to do too much. They have set impossible goals for themselves. They are expecting to create overnight life changes that would reasonably take a year or two, and maybe longer for those battling ADD.

It's better to choose one thing, just one small step you can work on, over the next two months. Then try another step. Then another. In a year you will have taken five or six positive steps toward a better life. That's far better than crashing and burning in the first week.

We have appreciated the movie *What About Bob?*—in which Bill Murray plays a man dealing with emotional problems. Bob is told that he must not try to recover all at once, that he must take "baby steps"—and we see him walking out of the office, putting one foot in front of the other, edging his way forward. It's a funny scene, and a poignant one. As an old Chinese saying goes, "Every journey begins with just one step."

4. Coping aids. Find a system to remember appointments and obligations. This is critical in our demanding society. How can you juggle the assignments you have from work or school, your

185

responsibilities with children or other family members, social activities, lunch or dinner get-togethers, medical appointments, and so on? Write it all down and then get into the habit of referring to your appointment book. Many people use some type of weekly or monthly calendar with a "to do" list. This can be especially helpful if important long-term goals and steps to accomplish such goals are included. Or, if these options are impossible for you, find some other system that works.

Many adults with ADD use their creativity to cope with their disorganized lives. One of the most creative coping methods we've seen was used by a client who had severe ADD and was unable to follow a schedule. This was especially difficult for him because he was in the sales business, which required him to attend to various meetings on a regular basis. He was charming, personable, well-liked and did an excellent job — when he remembered to show up for appointments. But, of course, his erratic attendance was a major problem.

He had tried numerous time management schedule books. Only he would lose them. Or he would forget to look at his schedule. He was at his wits' end. As a creative alternative, he began to wear a beeper. The office would call and tell him when and where to go next. That way he didn't need to follow a schedule. That system worked quite well for him — as long as he remembered to wear the beeper!

Obviously, time management is also a problem for some people without ADD, but the problem is entirely different for the ADDer. Time, in general, seems to be somewhat elusive for those with ADD. It's an abstract concept, separated from their daily lives. Time seems indefinite, infinite, and unable to be sliced into neat one-hour components. When those with ADD are beginning to use a calendar, it is always challenging and effective to break a long-term project into small, manageable steps and write those into their schedule.

November	Long-Term Goal: Clean out basement	Monday Nov. 6 thru Sunday Nov. 12

Monday, November 6		Thursday, November 9	
8 Sort items on	1	8 Drop off donated	1
9 floor:	2	9 items at	2
10 — Trash	3	charity. 10	3
11 — Donate	4	11	4
— Give away to friends			
— Save			
12 7:30—9:00pm	5	12	5

Tuesday, November 7		Friday, November 10	
8 Sort items on	1	8 Take giveaway	1
9 shelves and desk:	2	9 items to work	2
10 — Trash	3	10	3
11 — Donate	4	11	4
— Give away			
12 — Save 7:30—9:00pm	5	12 7:00pm Take box of clothes to Bridge Club	5

Wednesday, November 8		Saturday, Nov. 11	Sunday, Nov. 12
8 Take out all	1	9:00—Noon	
9 trash!	2	—Sort and stack remaining boxes.	Done!!
10	3	—Clean/Vacuum basement.	Watch game as reward.
11	4		
12	5		

Once I (Michele) asked a client to do a five- to ten-minute presentation on his experiences with ADD. After fifteen minutes I had to interrupt him because he kept on talking with no sign of abating. This in itself was an instructive moment: He commented that it was ridiculous to give a person with ADD a five- to ten-minute time frame, because he had no sense of time!

Allow time each day to organize your next day. Many waste a great deal of time because they fail to plan. Of course this is good advice for anyone, but for those with ADD, it's a necessity. Too many attractive distractions await those with ADD. Unless you have a track to follow, you will certainly get lost.

The computer stores are full of new items designed to help organize your time. (Steer clear of the game section, though — a sure distraction!) There are numerous calendars, to-do lists, address books, note organizers, etc. These packages generally cost between thirty and one hundred dollars. Examples include: Windows Calendar, Windows Cardfile, Lotus Organizer, and Day-Timer Organizer.

There are also voice beeping watches with multiple time settings, and voice recordings to prompt you. There are answering machines with a "memo" function for you to record messages to yourself. There are even key chains with mini-recorders enclosed, so you can record things you don't want to forget.

Take time to explore the technological advances available to see if you find something that may be helpful for you.

5. Procrastination. Procrastination has many root causes. For some people, it's a desire for perfection, a fear of failure, or an unconscious desire to sabotage one's own work. A person with ADD, however, procrastinates for different reasons— a difficulty understanding the reality of time, the "expensiveness" of sustained attention, and the lack of "activation" for new efforts.

If this is a problem for you, we bring you a simple message:

Decrease procrastination today!

We're not going to tell you to stop procrastinating entirely, because we're sure you've heard that before and tried that before, and failed too many times. So, for now, just try to procrastinate less. And you can start tomorrow. (Just kidding. You need to start today.)

If you usually wait to begin a work project or school assignment until the night before it's due, try to begin the *day* before. Remember, success is often measured by small steps.

Maybe someday you will put an end to your procrastination. Someday. But today you can do one small thing to *decrease* it.

SPACE

Space . . . the final frontier. No, not that kind of space. There's plenty of that. We're talking about a very limited space. The space on top of your desk. The space in your file cabinet. Or the space in your closet. There never seems to be enough space to store all the stuff we think we need. Part of getting organized is using the finite space we have more efficiently.

189

Everything has its place. To function in a fairly anxiety-free state, you need to have a place for most things. It will help simplify matters if you learn to keep certain items in certain places.

To do this, you need to establish a routine for the use of your space. For example, when you come home, place your keys on the key hook by the door. Once this becomes established as a habit, it will eliminate the morning stress of "Where are my keys? I'm going to be late!" The key hook will become the space for keys.

The same principle can work for papers. Bills, and only bills, could go into a basket on the kitchen counter. Other forms of paperwork, things that require some action other than payment, could be placed into a file or slot holder, whereas papers that you just wish to read at your leisure could be in a second file or slot, and items to file could be placed into a third file or slot.

This type of rough sorting would enable you to keep track of the important papers in your life. In the office, a similar type of rough sorting system could be developed.

Storage Containers. Use of files and a file cabinet or file storage container is also extremely helpful for those who struggle with organization. There are numerous storage containers available in office supply stores. It is well worth a trip to wander through the store and see what type of storage systems may work to simplify your particular organizational needs.

Storage containers work because they get things out of your way. A file will not distract you, and it will not clutter your space if it's sitting in a cabinet somewhere. Proper labeling of file drawers or boxes will help you retrieve files when you need them.

Space Is Finite, Stuff Is Not. Deal with the reality of space. It is important to realize the limits of space when you make decisions of what to keep and what to discard. Although it may be useful some day to look up an article from a magazine from ten years ago, it is unlikely you will remember where you saw the article, and even more unlikely that you would be able to retrieve the article when you need it. A local library would be a much better resource for finding such information. How many people do you know who have saved years' worth of certain magazines, hoping to use them some day, but never touching them again?

Periodically review the items taking up space and make sure they are still important enough to deserve the space they take up. Don't hesitate to throw things away or donate them to a thrift store. Think in terms of each item "paying rent" for the space it uses up. Does its value to you make up for the "rent" it has to pay?

Some homes do an annual "spring cleaning" in which unneeded "junk" is discarded or sold in a yard sale (to clutter someone else's space for a while). You might want to establish a regular evaluation of stuff and space. Less stuff is easier to manage.

STUFF

Obviously, our space is often cluttered because we have too much stuff in it. Therefore space management goes hand in hand with stuff management. ADDers tend to be pack rats, collecting things they have little use for. It's that same "can't say no" principle. Some ADDers can't say no to an impulse or distraction, others can't say no to a cute piece of junk in their basement because of the endless creative possibilities associated with it.

1. Spend fifteen minutes a day decreasing clutter. Make time each day or at least each week to organize your stuff. It would be great if your piles of paper would learn to organize themselves, but that won't happen. The longer you delay, the larger those piles will become.

But here's the secret: You don't have to clear the whole pile all at once. Just stay a step ahead of the stuff. Most people accumulate about ten minutes worth of stuff (junk mail, unneeded objects, magazines they'll never read, etc.) a day. That is, it would take about ten minutes each day to deal with each day's new stuff. If you devote just fifteen minutes each day to organizing the stuff you have accumulated, you'll chip away at those piles. In a week or two, you may even see the surface of your desk.

"But I don't have fifteen minutes a day!"

We hear you. But consider how much time you spend looking for stuff each day. Consider the anxiety that search creates, not to mention the family conflict, late fees from overdue bills, or missed deadlines. This is like the old oil filter commercial, "You can pay me now or pay me later." You've got that fifteen minutes a day, you just have to harness it.

2. Use bright colors or enticing designs. It may be easier and more enticing to work with your stuff if you use bright colors and/or interesting containers. Use files of different colors for different types of papers—work is orange, home is yellow, bills are red, and so on.

3. Cut down on your reading material. Many ADDers have stacks of magazines and newspapers they haven't read. They intend to read them someday, but they never will.

If that's the case with you, cut off this problem at the source. Cancel some subscriptions. If you get a daily newspaper, *maybe* you'd be all right with Sunday only. If you get several magazines, think about which ones you really need (or really read). Why couldn't you go to a library once a month to read the others?

Monitor your use of book, CD, or video clubs. Often those cards don't get sent back and the products come whether you want them or not. Then they just add to your clutter. It might be best to drop out of the club and go to a store for what you really want.

4. Make a list before you shop. On impulse, ADDers often buy things they don't need. Then the stuff sits around collecting dust, but you don't want to throw it out because you spent good money on it.

Make a shopping list before you shop—and stick to it. That will help to keep you from filling your home with white elephants.

5. Handle papers no more than twice. Some success experts tell executives to handle papers *once.* That is, they should decide on each thing immediately and pass it on for appropriate action. That's impractical for those of us who aren't CEOs, and yet many ADDers have piles of papers they've looked at again and again and again.

Use those sticky memo notes. (Have a supply handy.) If you are putting papers in a pile "for future consideration," make sure each one has a note on it saying what needs to be done or decided. That way you won't need to reread all those papers and you can get rid of them faster.

6. Give yourself a "throwaway budget." Some people hang on to major pieces of junk because they feel these pieces are worth something. An old toaster. That Veg-o-matic in the closet. An old Commodore computer. They never use these things, but maybe someday they will. (Right!)

Here's an idea. Ask yourself, "How much is it worth to have an uncluttered environment?" Set a dollar figure on that. Five hundred dollars? A thousand? In terms of your peace of mind, and the efficiency of your life, how much is that worth to you?

Write that figure down at the top of a piece of paper. That's your "throwaway budget." Then start looking at your old junk. If you threw away your toaster and decided down the road that you needed a new one, how much would one cost? Write that down and subtract it from your "budget" figure. How much would a new Veg-o-matic cost you if you needed one? Subtract that, too. And so on.

You probably don't really need to set aside that money, because you'll probably never need to replace those old objects. But in your mind, you're putting a value on an uncluttered home and charging the replacement cost of your old junk against it. Which is really more important to you? That may give you the push you need to toss that junk or donate it to a worthy cause.

In summary, ADDers often need to learn basic organizational skills. You may have tried various methods in the past and failed. But now that you know about ADD, you may cut yourself some slack, and allow yourself a little more time to develop those organizational habits. If you are now on medication, you should also have a renewed focus that will help you apply those organizational methods.

It is important to try again. Don't be discouraged if you are not successful on your first few tries. Disorganization may have become a habit for you, but habits can be changed. One small step at a time.

JUST THE FACTS

- It is not a lack of knowing what to do that causes ADDers difficulty with organization. It is the inability to do what they know they should and could do.

- The inconsistent ability to remain organized and perform tasks creates much frustration and leads to poor self-esteem for many adults with ADD.

- Inconsistency of attention is still something of a mystery to researchers. Some explain it as "disinhibition," an inability to reject distractions. Others see a lack of "activation," gearing up for a new task. Both may result from the high "expense" of sustained attention for the ADDer.

- There are many specific ways of organizing your self, space, and stuff, including:

SELF

- Structure your environment/routine

- Practice prioritizing—first things first

- Break tasks into small steps and be realistic about the pace for change

- Devise a creative system to remember appointments and obligations

(continued)

- Allow time to plan your day in advance

- Procrastinate less

SPACE

- Identify specific places for important items (keys, bills, etc.)

- Use functional storage containers

- Regularly evaluate the immediate value of the stuff taking up your limited space

- Don't hesitate to throw away or donate stuff from time to time

STUFF

- Take fifteen minutes each day to decrease clutter

- Use bright colors and interesting containers

- Cut down on your reading material

- Make a list before you shop

- Handle papers no more than twice

- Ask yourself, "How much is it worth to have an uncluttered environment?" and give yourself a "throwaway budget"

NOTES
1. From the video *ADHD in Adults* and the accompanying program manual *ADHD in Adults* (New York: Guilford Press, 1994).
2. *Chadder* (Spring/Summer 1993). Reference referred to in this article: T.E.Brown and G.D. Gammon "*Attention-Activation Disorder in Hi-IQ Underachievers*," Abs. Proceedings of American Psychiatric Association, 145th Annual Meeting, Washington, D.C., May 1992.
3. Kate Kelly and Peggy Ramundo, *You Mean I'm Not Lazy, Stupid or Crazy?* (Cincinnati, OH: Tyrell and Jerem Press, 1993).

CHAPTER FOURTEEN

LEARNING

ANDREW* WAS CLEARLY NOT *working up to his potential. What frustrated his parents was that he had such promise, yet he had flunked out of two colleges. He seemed very smart, but somehow he just couldn't apply himself to college tasks.*

In frustration, Andrew saw a counselor. The counselor suspected ADD and made a referral for an evaluation. He was diagnosed with ADD. Treatment involved medication as well as counseling and education for Andrew and his family.

Now Andrew is doing well in his second semester in college. The treatment didn't make his ADD go away, but it gave him the push he needed to get ahead of it. He still needs to structure his time more than most college students do, but he has learned how to do this. For instance, he goes to the library every Monday night to study. Every Monday night, without fail. He knows that if he skips a Monday study time, he probably won't make it up.

Andrew has learned to break down his assignments into pieces and plan a schedule that gives him time to do each piece. He also takes his language lab independently, so he can replay a session if needed and go at his own pace.

In addition, Andrew continues in counseling. He has been working through many issues related to his self-esteem and interpersonal relationships.

• ◆ •

Every ADDer we know has had trouble in learning situations. Many drop out of school or switch to less challenging schools or courses of study. Since ADD affects the information a person takes in, it has a drastic impact on his or her ability to learn.

What Is Learning?

There are many tasks involved in the learning process. First, a person *takes in information,* usually by hearing or seeing a presentation of it.

Second, a person *sifts through the information received,* keeping that which is important and allowing the rest to be forgotten. This aspect of learning is often overlooked, but "selective forgetting" is actually a key part of the process. If we didn't do this, we would be overwhelmed with the amount of data we receive.

Third, a person *retains the important information.* Short-term memory happens naturally, while long-term memory may involve some effort at memorizing the material.

Finally, a person *retrieves the information* at the appropriate time. Many of us have had the embarrassing experience of knowing that we know something—a person's name, for instance —but not being able to recall it. In such cases, the information is actually there, stored somewhere in our brains, but the neural signposts

200

leading us to its location have faded.

The ADDer can have difficulty in any or all of these aspects of the learning process.

TAKING IN INFORMATION

The first problem the ADDer has is simply in receiving information. Because of the lack of attention, a lot of data never gets into the brain at all. The ADDer is frequently distracted by other noises, movements, even thoughts. Competing noises or thoughts seem equally attractive to the brain, so it's hard for the ADDer to filter out distractions and gather the important information being presented.

ADDers have special difficulty attending to *auditory* information — lectures, seminars, verbal directions, and so on. Visual stimuli are more attractive, easier for the ADDer to follow.

As we have already indicated, the ADDer's life is filled with gaps — we've called them "blinks" — and so he or she will tend to get only part of the information presented.

Those with ADD also have difficulty *listening and taking notes at the same time*, as in a lecture or seminar situation. Many people take this ability for granted, but it requires regular shifting of attention from the lecture to the paper and back again. Every shift is a potential off-ramp on the ADDer's personal information highway. Tasks that require divided attention are usually quite hard for people with ADD.

Many adults with ADD also have trouble *reading*. Some of this may stem from early school experiences. Often a child who falls behind early in reading skills — due to ADD or some other learning problem — has to play catch-up all his life.

201

But reading can also be a less rewarding activity than watching something or even listening—especially if you're reading textbooks. Remember how much effort it takes for the ADDer to pay attention. With reading, there is no visual movement or ongoing sound to help draw the ADDer's attention to the material—just the words on the page. Thus it takes extra energy to read and extra motivation to even *start* a reading assignment.

Reading also requires a certain amount of consistent mental participation—visualizing or reframing the material one reads. But this is, in a way, a split task—reading and visualizing, reading and visualizing—and the ADDer can get lost in the transitions. We've heard several ADDers talk about reading and rereading the same page and not being able to get through it. It's not that the information is too heavy for them, it's just that their minds go off on other journeys before they finish the page.

Reading takes a long time. Thus it requires sustained attention, something that's very difficult for the ADDer. And in many situations, reading is progressive. That is, page 47 is based on things you've read on page 46, and so on. If an ADDer "blinks" on page 46 (perhaps not even realizing it), she will have a hard time understanding page 47.

All of these factors make reading an especially challenging task for those with ADD. And, since reading is fundamental to education, this creates learning problems for many ADDers.

There's one other setback in the process of taking in information—*emotional self-talk*. As we have seen, ADDers face great difficulty in this first aspect of learning, and therefore the whole process is fraught with anxiety. "Can I do this? Maybe not. Probably not. And what will happen if I don't?"

A non-ADDer just picks up a book and reads, or sits down at a lecture and takes notes. But the ADDer has a whole emotional monologue going on, *and this can be a source of distraction.* It's like having a second television on in the same room.

Because many people with ADD have poor self-esteem, this emotional monologue is usually negative: "I'll never be able to do this." This often becomes a self-fulfilling prophecy.

Psychologist Albert Ellis talks about the process of "awfulizing"—making a situation more awful than it really is by imagining all sorts of disasters. "I can't read this, and because I can't, I'll flunk out of school, and then I'll only be able to get a fast-food job flipping burgers, so I won't ever be able to buy a house. . . ." So, while you should be on page 47, your mind is on skid row somewhere, collecting unemployment checks.

In a few cases, even positive self-talk can be a distraction. "Hey, I'm doing pretty well. I'm following this lecture perfectly. If I keep this up, I'll be able to go on for a Master's degree, and maybe teach in some comfy community college and . . . ." And you've lost it again.

The point is that learning is an issue for ADDers, and the emotional response to this issue can take center stage in one's mind, making it even more difficult to learn.

SIFTING THROUGH INFORMATION

ADDers find it hard to decide what is important and what is not. People without ADD regularly weigh the merits of the information they receive, but ADDers say yes to everything. It all comes in and it all gets equal billing.

The ADDer listens to a lecture but also hears someone coughing in the back row. The non-ADDer hears it too, but quickly decides, "Oh, that's just someone coughing. It's more important to listen to the lecture." The ADDer, however, gives equal weight to the cougher and the professor. Add seven other background noises, and the ADDer has a lot to contend with.

Helen tells of her attempts to listen to college lectures in the days before she got treatment for ADD. "I would count the number of tiles in the ceiling, the number of red shirts in the room, the number of steps in the lecture hall." Every detail clamored for her attention.

Non-ADDers routinely sift important information from unimportant, even when it comes from the same source, but ADDers don't do this well. The lecturer may tell an amusing legend about how Euclid came up with a certain theorem. The non-ADDer knows that the story is just a story — the important thing is the theorem. But the ADDer takes it all in. The ADDer places just as much value on the color of Euclid's toga as on the variables in his equations.

That might be fine if a person could remember all of it and instantly access any detail needed. But we can only hold so many details in our brains, and it's confusing to sift through a lot of trivia to get to the important stuff. Ironically, the learning problem of the ADDer is not that he does not get enough information, but that he gets too much!

In this way, the ADDer's brain can be a lot like his or her home or office — cluttered. If you took every piece of mail you've received in the last year and just piled it all on your desk, how would you ever find the important things? Non-ADDers learn to throw out the junk right away so it doesn't clutter their desks. Similarly, non-ADDers sift out the unimportant information they receive so it doesn't clutter their brains. But ADDers have trouble throwing things away, whether it's junk mail or "junk data."

As a result, people with ADD often feel overloaded. There is too much to deal with, so they just shut down. At that point, they can miss out on important new information because they've been overloaded by unimportant details.

RETAINING THE IMPORTANT INFORMATION

ADDers often have trouble storing information. Even though they may hear or see the information, it may not get to short- or long-term memory. Because the data is not sifted, there is too much to handle and the memory quickly fills up. It's something like a computer whose memory gets packed with video games. When you have an important file to save, you get an "out of memory" message.

Everyone's memory fades through time. A person may recall an event that happened years earlier but may remember only its high points — the most important details. However, the ADDer's memories are not that well organized. They may remember the color tie the boss wore on the day the job was given, but forget the job assignment.

RETRIEVING INFORMATION

Like a person searching for a birth certificate in a pile of store fliers and magazine promotions, the ADDer may have a hard time retrieving

205

something that has been learned. This is one of the more embarrassing aspects of the disorder. ADDers get labeled as absent-minded, airheads, space cadets, and so on.

This is especially frustrating after the person has expended so much effort to learn the material in the first place. When you study for an exam every night for a week, you want that effort to pay off. Sadly, for many ADDers, it doesn't. Regularly they tell us they have to study three or four times as much as their non-ADD classmates, and still they struggle.

It's a bit like pouring water into a cup with a narrow opening at the top and a crack in the bottom. Even when you succeed, with great effort, in pouring water in, it leaks out. The cup is not doing its job. In the same way, the ADDer's brain is not only making it difficult to get information in, it is also letting it leak out.

Organizational Difficulties

In Chapter 13 we discussed the difficulties ADDers have with organizing their lives. This can hinder the learning process significantly. ADDers often lose things. And if you can't find your lists, keys, supplies, and so on, it sets you back.

Since time management is also a struggle for those with ADD, they are often late for appointments or meetings, or they forget about them entirely. They forget to prepare until it's too late. The day before a project is due, they suddenly decide to start working on it.

Certainly there are non-ADDers who are also disorganized and poor time managers. But the ADDer has so many other factors working against him or her that missing a class could be disastrous.

It is tough to play catch-up all the time.

There are also ADDers who have worked hard to organize themselves or those who don't have difficulty in this area.

Learning Disabilities

Many with ADD also have a specific learning disability in addition to the ADD. Wait, you say, isn't ADD a learning disability itself? Not technically. There are strong relationships between ADD and learning disabilities, but ADD itself has not been classified in that category.

A learning disability is a psychological disorder that has to do with "using language, spoken or written, which may manifest itself in an imperfect ability to listen, think, speak, read, write, spell, or do mathematical calculations. The term includes such conditions as perceptual handicaps, brain injury, minimal brain dysfunction, dyslexia, and developmental aphasia."[1]

So there may be *other* learning problems that follow an ADDer through childhood and into adulthood. Dr. Larry Silver states, "Of all the children and adolescents with ADHD, it is estimated that between 50% and 80% will also have a learning disability."[2]

TIPS FOR LEARNING BETTER
Many schools offer classes in study skills, and some even offer specialized help for ADD or learning-disabled students. But there are several strategies we can mention here that may help keep the ADDer on track in a learning environment. *(continued)*

207

1. Tape your classes, lectures or seminars.
Then you can replay the tape later to fill in the
gaps.

2. Get notes from someone else. Classmates,
friends, coworkers, professors, or speakers
may be able to supply you with notes so that
you can listen without the distraction of taking
notes yourself. If you explain your ADD, they
should be happy to accommodate you—you're
not being lazy, you're being smart.

3. Use a study group or tutor. You need help
differentiating important from unimportant
information. Others can help you with this.
Even if it's not an organized study group or
tutoring session, try to review the content of
the class or seminar with others.

4. Use medication. Even those who resist taking medication on a full-time basis find that it
can help greatly in learning situations. You could
plan "medicated mornings" and schedule your
classes (or toughest work projects) for the times
when the medication is having its fullest effect.

5. Establish peer accountability. Since motivation is often a problem for the ADDer, get
someone to check on you periodically, just to
make sure you are doing what you said you
wanted to be doing.

6. Get counseling. A good counselor can teach
you new learning skills, help repair your self-
esteem, and reduce your negative self-talk. We
like the comment a parent made recently on a
TV talk show: "Pills are not skills." Medication
helps, but specific learning skills still need to
be retaught.

Accommodations for the ADDer

Employers, teachers, and administrators can make "reasonable accommodations" that may help the ADD sufferer immensely. Remember that ADDers are not dumb. They just have difficulty with the normal pace and style of gathering information. The following measures may help get around that.

- After meetings or classes, make notes available.

- Repeat the key points of a lecture or meeting.

- Give all assignments in written form, not just orally.

- Set intermediate deadlines so that part of the project should be done by this date, the next part by that date, and so on.

- Allow for alternative testing, including essay tests, oral reports, or skills tests. Normal written tests do not always fairly assess the ADDer's knowledge of a subject.

- Allow untimed tests. ADDers may take longer to summon the information, but it's there.

- Take stand-up, walk-around breaks in classes or meetings. (In business, try short stand-up meetings.)

JUST THE FACTS

ADDers have learning difficulties in the following areas:

• Taking in information;

• Sifting through information;

• Retaining the important information;

• Retrieving information;

• Organizational difficulties that affect the learning process;

• Possible additional learning disabilities.

• The ADDer can take responsibility to tape meetings or classes, get notes from others, use a tutor, and seek treatment for ADD with medication and counseling.

• Companies, teachers, and schools can make certain accommodations for those with ADD to make the best use of their potential and overcome some learning problems.

NOTES
1. Federal Law: Education for All Handicapped Children (Public Law 94-142), cited in Larry Silver, *Dr. Larry Silver's Advice to Parents on Attention Deficit Hyperactivity Disorder* (Washington, DC: American Psychiatric Press, Inc., 1993), p. 42.
2. Silver, p. 8.

CHAPTER FIFTEEN

RELATIONSHIPS

PAUL AND MARCY got married about ten years ago. It was Paul's third marriage, Marcy's first. They met, fell in love, and married within just a few months. Marcy was elated—but she didn't know this had been a pattern for Paul's previous relationships. He would dive impulsively into a relationship but soon grow bored.

The difference with this marriage, however, was the fact that they had a child fairly quickly. Now, even though they both are openly dissatisfied with the relationship, they stay together, primarily because of their three children.

According to Marcy, Paul tends to be very self-centered. He has a difficult time understanding other people's perceptions and can't follow conversations that involve more than one person at a time. He doesn't seem to pick up on social nuances and can only focus on one thing at a time. Therefore, the focus is usually on himself.

This self-focus is a blind spot for Paul, and a chief complaint for Marcy. She sees his

*selfishness as deliberate. She gets frustrated
explaining to him what she expects from him and
what needs to be done around the house, yet
there never seems to be any change for the better.
"It's like having a fourth child," Marcy explains. "I
know he's not stupid, and yet he just doesn't get
it. He's frequently late, insensitive when we're
with others, and he rarely does anything to help
around the house." It is hard for her to fight her
feelings of resentment toward him.*

*According to Paul, he's not the problem —
Marcy is just too critical and doesn't understand
him. He is oblivious to what he is doing wrong,
but admits to being somewhat disorganized.
Paul feels that the marriage is in a rut and holds
out little hope that it will ever change. He admits
that he is bored with the relationship, but that
he'll stay around as long as the kids are in the
home.*

*Paul also looks for excitement in other activ-
ities and hobbies. His pattern is to get very
involved in a new activity and impulsively pursue
it, only to abandon it and move on to something
else within a few months. For example, he got
interested in photography and bought scads of
expensive equipment. About six months later, he
lost interest. Now all of the stuff lies on a shelf
collecting dust.*

Yes, Paul has ADD.

• ◆ •

Problems in relationships abound in the adult who
has ADD, but it is difficult to identify specific problems you might be experiencing, since the symptoms you have will depend on the type of ADD you
have. Some ADDers are impulsive and hyperactive,

212

others distracted. So some of the following descriptions will fit you to a T, others will sound completely foreign.

"OF COURSE I'M LISTENING"

One common complaint of ADDers (and those who know them) is their apparent difficulty in listening to others. Blame it on their distractibility, their impulsiveness, or their overactivity, but no matter how you slice it, ADDers find it hard to stay with a conversation. This may not be apparent at first, because new acquaintances are always a little more interesting and that newness helps to hold the ADDer's attention. But once a real relationship sets in, watch out; that's when the ADDer may become bored, distracted, and aloof.

An ADDer will commonly fidget while someone else is talking, interrupt in the middle of a crucial point, or change the subject abruptly. In some cases, the ADDer may just walk away from a conversation.

Obviously, this can hurt any significant relationship. The difficulty is most apparent in the adult ADDer's relationships with other adults or older teenagers, since these tend to be more intense and complex than interactions with children.

One father with ADD explained it this way: "When my children were little, I could get on the floor with them and play. Their attention spans were short and so was mine. It made for a fun time. But now my kids are older. They want to talk about their music, their MTV, their boyfriends or girlfriends, and their problems. I have a real hard time listening well to any of it. Relationships that were once above average are now nonexistent."

In adult encounters, people with ADD are at a tremendous disadvantage. They generally don't pick up subtle nuances, have difficulty following extended or complicated conversations, and may not be interested in the things others want to talk about. It's true that many people have trouble being good conversationalists, whether they have ADD or not. But ADDers have to work especially hard at listening.

"HERE TODAY, GONE TOMORROW"

The impulsiveness of the ADDer is well documented. We saw this in the story of Paul and Marcy at the beginning of this chapter. Paul jumped impulsively into the relationship (as was his pattern) and then lost interest after a while. He had the same tendency with his hobbies and his jobs.

Dating the ADDer can be a roller-coaster experience. He or she may seem very interested in pursuing you one day and then be gone the next. The ADDer's interest may even wax and wane like the moon. This can lead to a frustrating and unhealthy relationship, especially if the non-ADD partner goes to great lengths to "win over the one with ADD." The ADDer is not playing hard to get; the ADDer *is* hard to get.

A marriage can be the same way. One woman explained: "When we were dating it was great because he was so intense and so exciting. I felt like life was one big adventure with Jack. I never knew what was coming next—camping, the theater, skydiving. He was so unpredictable. But then, as the relationship settled down, I felt like he was bored with me, and jumping on to something else. Our relationship was built on doing things and having fun. But when it came to having a meaningful dialogue, Jack wasn't there. Now, after four years of marriage and a child, Jack has moved on to more exciting pursuits."

Cynics might say that most men and some women are like this anyway. That may be true. But the impulsive ADDer has a special problem in this area. Research indicates that ADDers have a higher rate of divorce, substance abuse, and relational problems. They may also be more prone to affairs, irresponsible risk-taking, and self-destructive behaviors. All of these may be a result of their search for something new and more exciting.

Remember that ADD inhibits the ability to say no. That may help the ADDer say yes to a relationship (or another pursuit) too quickly, and then say yes to *another* relationship (or another pursuit) quickly.

Spouses of ADDers, like Marcy, may feel rejected, and understandably so. But the ADDer is not actually rejecting the current relationship; rather, he is accepting other pursuits that seem to "cost" less. Remember that sustained attention is *expensive* for the person with ADD. It takes a lot more effort to make a marriage work than it does to flit after some handy new romance. Of course, this part of an ADDer's disorder is no excuse for abandoning his or her commitments and responsibilities!

"I NEVER SAID THAT!"

Forgetfulness is another frequent complaint about the ADDer. This tendency can be the result of several ADD symptoms — distractibility, poor listening skills, lack of organization—or of weak memory skills.

This trait can be a great source of tension in an ADDer's relationships. Lateness or missed appointments can create resentment. "Things to do" lists get lost or ignored, and arguments break out over "I never said that" or "I never agreed to do that." The ADDer always seems to be a day late and a dollar short.

People close to an ADDer often assume he or she is deliberately lying or trying to squeeze out of a sticky situation. But when the scene is played out again and again, the other person may begin to wonder, "Is it me?" The ADDer can sound so convinced and sure of himself that it seems as if it must be someone else's fault.

The truth is, of course, that ADDers often *don't* remember. They may have spent ten minutes going over the shopping list, but that may have been a "blink," a time of distraction, and none of it stuck.

This pattern will continue to cause problems unless the ADDer acknowledges his or her memory weakness and spouses or friends arrive at an understanding of the problem. They need to act without judgment and the ADDer needs to act without pride. This way, "I never said that" can become "Did I say that?" And that can lead to "You must have forgotten. How can we help you remember next time?" The ADDer must work together with the people in his or her life to find ways to organize information and establish regular reminders.

"GET OFF MY CASE!"

Many ADDers are playing a game of subtle deception. They can get quite good at it. But trying to maintain that you have it together when you know you don't can be a source of tremendous pain for the ADDer. I've seen many who medicate their pain with alcohol, others who retreat from any emotional intimacy, and still others who flare up in a defensive rage when they are challenged.

The pain of such people is usually just below the surface, so anyone who pricks the skin at all may find a deep level of anger and frustration. Relationships may be characterized by heated arguments or by walls of avoidance. Any comment may be a battlefield, or else people are walking away from each other whenever they feel even the slightest pressure or challenge. You may be spitting fire at each other, or you may go through life feeling like you're walking on eggshells, not wanting to awaken the monster within.

When Marilyn first married Sam, she was drawn to his assertive confidence and apparent strength. But as she got closer, she found a man who could not stand to have anyone question him or challenge his thinking. Sam was trying to run several projects at once, and would jump from thing to thing. At first Marilyn marveled at how he seemed to handle it all. But then she learned the truth. He was not handling it. His money and business were really just a shell game — he was pretending to be someone he wasn't, pretending to have something that he didn't.

She loved him and wanted to support him, but when she tried to talk to him about it, he would deny that there was a problem and just walk away. If she pursued him, he became angry and sometimes violent. Over time Marilyn learned to let him go but lived with the frustration of not being able to get close to him. She stood by and watched as Sam became more and more frustrated, more and more angry, and increasingly isolated. Marilyn simply learned how to get out of his way.

• ◆ •

The problem with ADD-induced anger in relationships, whether openly expressed or hidden, is that the ADDer isn't really angry at the spouse or friend. In the heat of the moment it may seem that way, but the ADDer is really angry at *it*—at the ADD. The spouse or friend feels helpless and can respond in anger at being unfairly blamed.

When the anger is "stuffed" and not expressed, it festers. It can paralyze a relationship. Counseling can be crucial for a couple whose relationship has stagnated (or exploded) due to anger at ADD. Both parties must be allowed to express their frustrations honestly and healthily. The monster can be tamed.

"ALL ABOUT ME"

ADDers tend to be more self-focused than others. Some would interpret this behavior as selfish, but there's a moral judgment in that term that doesn't always apply.

As we have said, the ADDer has difficulty sustaining attention toward outside objects. It is expensive to pay attention, and that "expense" is hard to pay unless there are specific "rewards." What kind of rewards? Entertainment, excitement, interest, novelty.

Picture the couch potato watching TV with the

remote control in hand. When a show stops giving him anything new and exciting, he flicks to a different channel. If he finds a show on, say, basket-weaving in Uganda, he will move quickly past it — unless he happens to be a basket-weaver or unless he's from Uganda. We all find things that pertain to ourselves more interesting than ones that don't. In the ADDer's case, we can say those experiences, conversations, and people that focus on the particular interests and needs of the ADDer "pay off" — the attention is rewarded.

All of us are generally more interested in things that have to do with our own lives rather than in things outside our experience. But the ADDer has a greater imbalance in this area. It is much harder to pay attention to things outside the self and, comparatively, much easier to attend to self-related things. Therefore, the ADDer is more self-focused and can *seem* selfish to others.

A woman described her ADD husband this way: "He will sit and watch TV and never help out around the house unless I badger him. He forgets to take out the trash or to do any of the chores I ask him to do. He frequently will not show up or will be late to appointments that I make for us, like parent-teacher conferences or doctor's appointments for the kids. But he never seems to forget about the hunting trip with the guys or any trips he's interested in!"

Most people have an understanding of delayed gratification. We know that today's trip to the dentist may be painful, but we know that it will create long-term dental health — and so it's worth it. We don't like to do dishes, but we know that they'll just pile up until they get washed, and it's much easier to wash dishes before they get encrusted. We may

219

not enjoy hearing all the details of the story Mrs. Oshkosh is telling us, but we know that she'll be offended if we don't — and we don't want to risk the wrath of Mrs. Oshkosh!

But the ADDer lives in the moment. That long-term view is often not available. So the dishes will pile up and crust over and the ADDer will buy paper plates. But that does not mean the ADDer is selfish, just self-focused and moment-to-moment.

Of course, this behavior can wreak havoc in relationships, especially in marriages. Good marriages are built on rather equal participation, and if one partner feels that he or she is putting in 90 percent of the effort, resentment can grow. That spouse needs to insist on responsible participation by the ADDer, and perhaps developing some immediate-gratification methods may help. But most important, the partner must understand how *expensive* the attention is for the ADDer.

"IT'S ALL MY FAULT"

Many ADDers are plagued with a poor self-image, usually a result of years of underachievement and misunderstanding. Most ADDers have struggled through school, feeling dumb and lazy. These labels are often reinforced by teachers, parents, bosses, spouses and peers.

In an adult relationship, this poor self-image comes through in many ways, including insecurity, lack of confidence, overcompensation, and avoidance.

ADDers often seek jobs in occupations that are beneath them, desperately trying to avoid failure by lowering the stakes. They may do the same in dating relationships, dating "beneath themselves" in order to feel more competent. These relationships frequently self-destruct in time, only to be repeated again because the root issues are still there. We have seen this trait especially in women.

Andrea had a history of dating men that were all wrong for her. She was a very poor student, and in high school got into the wrong crowd, experimenting with drugs, sex, and alcohol. After high school, she meandered from job to job, relationship to relationship. Her parents finally got her to go to a counselor, who diagnosed ADD. The knowledge helped her to view herself in a better light, but she still had no confidence in her ability to return to college or to hold down a job. Her relationship pattern was also so deeply ingrained that she didn't know how to meet men without going to a bar or club. And of course, she always ended up with the same type.

For Andrea to change her unhealthy pattern, she first must do some work on her self-image. Medication may help her cognitive abilities, but repairing her psyche will take a lot more time and work.

•◆•

Spouses and friends may be frustrated by the low self-image of the ADDer. "Why don't you stand up for yourself?" This can have a spiral effect, as the ADDer berates himself for having a poor self-image and thus has a worse self-image.

ADDers can also overcompensate for a poor self-image by taking unwise risks, by bragging about great achievements (usually some future task that will "turn everything around for us"), or by denying the problems. These traits can also be hard to live with.

The answer, of course, is an honest appraisal of one's situation. Acceptance from spouse and friends is crucial, but the ADDer must also be encouraged to see the long, slow path toward healing and renewed confidence. That long-range vicw is not easy for the ADDer, but along with the proper treatment for ADD, he or she can embark on that journey.

"DON'T ROCK THE BOAT!"

Like many of the ADD symptoms, this characteristic may seem contradictory. Earlier we said that ADDers look for change and new challenges. But it is also true that many ADDers are resistant to change, and don't do well with transitions. We see this with minor changes, such as having to jump from task to task, as in the case of the receptionist who must handle four phone lines at one time. In order to get the job done, some ADDers track tightly into certain tasks and are thrown off when they have to take on a new assignment.

This resistance is also seen with major changes, such as a move to a new home or employment situation. Major moves create so many distractions that ADDers often fear being overwhelmed. Mentally, they can go on "overload" and shut down.

Since many ADDers structure their lives as a way of coping with their disorder, if you come along and disrupt that schedule or routine, it may throw off their whole day. In a work situation, they may ask others to put their requests in writing and to give them prior notice of any changes in their schedule. This may seem cold or arrogant, but in fact, it may be their way of keeping control of their lives.

In the normal give-and-take of marriage, flexibility is a plus. Some ADDers have none. A spouse can learn to work within the ADDer's coping methods. However, this inflexibility can extend to a resistance to dealing with important issues—and perhaps even seeking treatment for ADD. The ADDer fears the upheaval of the life he or she has so carefully arranged. In such cases, the caring spouse can work to replace fear with hope, always remembering that the decision to make positive changes is the responsibility of the one with ADD. A spouse can help, but improving the relationship is a mutual effort. A spouse must insist that the ADDer take his or her full responsibility.

How to Change for the Better

If you have ADD, and you are having trouble with your relationships, what can you do to improve things?

ONE: SEEK TREATMENT

This should go without saying by now, but it's essential. The best thing you can do to improve your relationships is to admit you have a problem with ADD and seek treatment for it, through counseling, medication, and behavior modification. You may be amazed at how many other things will fall into place.

TWO: ACCEPT YOURSELF

You may have had a history of failure, but that can change. You may have alienated friends and family, but you can now begin to undo some of that damage. You are not doomed to live a life of underachievement and misunderstanding. There is hope for you.

As you begin your journey toward wholeness, involving responsible ADD management, it's okay to be where you are. Don't scold yourself for not being two miles up the road. You're here now, and that's fine. You will get there, in time.

Because of ADD, you have probably done a lot of things that you aren't proud of. The restoration of your past relationships and/or the building of new relationships requires that you first learn to accept yourself.

THREE: DECIDE TO BE HONEST

You may have spent a lot of time hiding your problems. Now it's time to open up to the people closest to you. Admit the struggle you have had (and are having) with ADD. Ask for their help when you need it.

The first ingredient of any good relationship is *communication*. Communication leads to understanding. You need to explain your situation to the important people in your life. Help them to understand where you've been and where you want to go—with their help.

FOUR: GIVE GIFTS OF ATTENTION

It is expensive to pay attention to other people. Even if medication is helping you to focus, you have a lifetime of distraction that has taught you bad habits. It's still hard work to listen to people, even to your loved ones.

But what if you begin to look at attention as a precious gift you want to give to your spouse or to your children or to your friends? You would spend hard-earned money on flowers or jewelry or expensive video games. Will you spend some attention on these special people?

Get over that hurdle of always analyzing things according to "What's the payoff for me?" Bring some joy to others by paying attention.

FIVE: PRACTICE ACTIVE LISTENING

Listening is a skill that may take some time to learn. Here's one tip: Good listeners are active listeners, not passive listeners. Good listeners get involved in a conversation, prodding the speaker with pertinent questions. "What happened then?" "How did you feel about that?"

In the past, your mental activity would lead you *away* from the listening process. Now you need to rechannel your thoughts into words that go back *into* what the other person is saying. This will take some practice, but it will pay off in more satisfying relationships.

SIX: MAKE CONTRACTS

You may have tended to flit from one thing to another. With proper treatment, you will have less of a *need* to do that, but you may still have that *habit*.

It may help to commit to a particular project, hobby, or other pursuit for a period of time. If you take up photography, for instance, decide to stay with it for at least a year. Put regular reminders on your calendar. If you begin to clean up the basement, make a contract with your family in which you (and the others, perhaps) agree to keep working at this project for a month or until it's done, whichever comes first.

If you put these things in writing, it may help to curb your impulsivity. Keep your time commitments short at first, and then build them up. Keep your projects at reasonable levels of difficulty. Don't expect to repanel your living room in an hour.

SEVEN: ESTABLISH A SYSTEM TOGETHER

Work together with the people you live with and work with to set up organizational systems that will make life easier for everyone concerned. If you forget things, learn to write them down — even put a blackboard or dry-erase board on the wall so that everyone can be reminded of the tasks and terms agreed to.

If you need regular reminders on certain tasks, ask people for them. Establish with your spouse exactly when reminding becomes "nagging." The third reminder? The eighth? How many reminders do you need?

You may have some systems that you have developed to cope with your ADD, but you need to get other people into those systems, and set up new systems with them. They should be happy to do this, as long as they feel that the whole house or office will run more smoothly.

EIGHT: TAKE THE LONG VIEW

Expect to have setbacks along the way. You will slip into old habits from time to time, and this will disappoint you and the people closest to you. Don't give up hope. This is not a 100-yard sprint, but a marathon. You have plenty of time to pick yourself up and start moving again in the right direction.

It may help to ask your loved ones at various intervals, "How am I doing?" Ask them to compare your current behavior to a month ago, or a year ago.

Keep a journal. Even if you only get to it every week or so, it will help you a year from now to see how things were. It will give you bench marks with which to chart your progress as you step steadily toward healing and well-being.

How to Help an ADDer Change

If you live with or love someone who has ADD and want to help them change the way they interact in relationships, there are some things you can do, and other things you need to let go of.

1. Urge them to get treatment. You can't do this for them, but you can help to get information and make some contacts. Without proper treatment, the ADDer is likely to stay in denial and continue the patterns that frustrate you, no matter what you do. Amateur methods are not going to help much. You need professional guidance.

2. Stop managing the ADD for them. Although the following suggestions may seem to contradict this point, it's crucial to develop a certain philosophy of ADD management: It is not up to you to manage your loved one's ADD. It is his or her responsibility. You can bend and push and cajole and encourage, but ultimately the ADDer is responsible to deal with his or her problem.

3. Work out a system of organization together. Set up systems that will help you both remember what has been said and agreed to. Write things down. Establish places to put certain things, like keys. (See item seven, mentioned earlier on page 226.)

4. Repeat and remind. Understand that there are gaps in the ADDer's perception of conversations and events. Therefore, you may need to fill in the gaps from time to time. Repeat things without condemnation. Offer cheerful reminders. Give the ADDer a second chance at important information.

5. Appreciate the expense involved in paying attention. Reward even little bits of attention with love and appreciation. As we have said, it costs the ADDer a lot of energy to pay attention to something or someone for any length of time. If you understand this, it may make you grateful for the attention that is paid and less resentful of the attention that drifts away.

6. Establish an environment of encouragement. The ADDer requires patience, as you well know. Often, the people around the ADDer express nothing but judgment, disappointment, and pain. The ADDer's already low self-esteem sinks lower. The person withdraws all the more, hiding his or her symptoms rather than facing more embarrassment.

Encouragement is a fine art. It involves a lot of stroking, along with occasional kicks in the pants. It says, "I understand your difficulty," and at the same time, "I know you can do better." The ADDer needs to be applauded for efforts to manage and control ADD, but also needs to be held accountable for his or her behavior.

At the same time, there are some positive aspects of ADD that can be affirmed. Is your ADDer creative, forward-thinking, fun to be with? Then say so.

7. Get your needs met. People who love someone with ADD need to set up healthy boundaries. The ADDer is not your "project." Your success in life is not determined by whether or not you "cure" someone's ADD.

We hesitate to use the overused term *codependence,* but it can occur in ADD situations. You can get so wrapped up in the ADDer's problem that you ignore your own needs. Communicate these needs to the ADDer. You may be surprised at how these needs get met. Or the ADDer may ignore you. If so, establish a life of your own, with activities and friends that satisfy your needs.

In any relationship, you need to ask yourself, "What is this relationship about? Is it about me? Is it about the other person? Is it about some problem that he (or she) has or that I have? Or is it about *us*?" Good relationships are about "us." ADD can easily shift the balance in a relationship. You need to do all you can, in love, to shift that balance back.

JUST THE FACTS

People with ADD usually have at least some of the following relational difficulties:

- Problems in listening to others

- Impulsively jumping from task to task, or person to person; easily bored

- Forgetfulness

- Easily frustrated, leading sometimes to angry outbursts

(continued)

229

- Tendency to be self-focused, which can appear selfish

- Low self-image and insecurity in relationships

- Difficulty with transitions and change

These problems can be lessened through communication, honesty, mutual effort, and proper treatment of ADD. Both people in a relationship need to understand the problems of ADD and allow for a healthy give-and-take of feelings. The ADDer must be held accountable for his or her actions. Patience, acceptance, and encouragement can go a long way toward helping the ADDer make gradual, positive changes in his or her behavior.

CHAPTER SIXTEEN

WORK

AS WE CONSIDER the experience of the ADDer at work, we're actually encountering two problems at once: learning difficulties and relationship difficulties. The workplace is, of course, a place of learning and doing. The same challenges that face an ADDer in school can extend to the workplace— blanking out when certain tasks are explained, for instance. But the workplace also has many relationships, and coworkers can have some of the same frustrations about the ADDer that spouses and friends have.

Let's focus on ten particular problems that occur with some frequency among ADDers in the workplace.

1. Difficulty with specific tasks
2. The lure of the "other"
3. Missed appointments
4. Impulsive decision making
5. Rigid patterns
6. The need for a cooperative environment
7. Failure mentality

8. Frustration and anger
9. Ignorance of office politics
10. Hyperactivity

PROBLEM ONE: DIFFICULTY WITH SPECIFIC TASKS

Sometimes ADDers excel at their work. Many of the positive aspects of ADD can be harnessed to benefit an employer. But there is a maddening inconsistency—one day the ADDer is a star employee, the next day he or she is on the ropes.

We have already discussed many of the learning issues that affect the performance of those with ADD. Let's briefly examine the major ones here.

Sometimes ADDers miss important details of a new assignment. They "blink" while the directions are being given, and so they're not sure how to do a job. Worse, they don't know what they have missed. They think they got it all, but they didn't.

ADDers can take two or three times as long as others to do a project. They tend to be hard workers, and they may stay overtime to get things done, but it takes them longer. They are constantly reviewing what they've read because it didn't stick the first time. Or they have to recalculate a column of numbers because they drifted off.

People with ADD are especially vulnerable in transitions. Stopping one thing to start another is a difficult process. And yet those transitions may happen many times in a workday. The ADDer needs extra time to key into a new project.

Marsha was successful in her job, working for a man who was probably ADD also. She answered his phones and typed up letters for him. Even

232

though he just kept spouting out idea after idea, which tended to drive her crazy, while the business remained small, she was able to handle it. But then one of his ideas hit it big!

The business took off. New employees were hired. Six phone lines were added, and Marsha was positioned to grow with the company. She and her boss had meetings about profit sharing, stock ownership, and options to purchase future shares. But she felt lost in all of the business growth. Others told her what a great opportunity this was for her, but she longed for the days when it was just a small business with two employees.

Marsha was not able to handle the transitions, the phone calls, and the hectic pace. As new people were added, people who could thrive in such an environment, Marsha couldn't keep up. She gradually lost her place in the pecking order.

Discouraged, frustrated, and feeling left out, she quit her job. While her boss was sad to see her go, he viewed her departure as a necessary loss. He needed to surround himself with people who could handle the pace—those who could follow through on his creative ideas, and his hectic schedule.

•◆•

This story demonstrates two opposite job situations for people with ADD. The boss had the freedom to dream and scheme, surrounding himself with people who would deal with the details. His ADD may have helped him in his work.

But Marsha was at a level where she had to mind the details. When the business grew, there were too many details. She hit her personal "job ceiling."

This ceiling is an all-too-common reality for ADDers. They see where they want to go, they dream of the possibilities, but they can't get there. Interestingly, it seems that middle management is an especially troublesome swamp for ADDers. Some people, like Marsha's boss, manage to vault over that whole area. They become executives or entrepreneurs by being in the right place at the right time with the right idea. But others, like Marsha, remain chained to the lower rungs of the corporate ladder. They can do limited tasks very well, but without effective ADD treatment, they find it difficult to take on multi-task responsibilities.

PROBLEM TWO: THE LURE OF THE "OTHER"

The ADDer tends to see other things to do. The coffee needs to be made, the paper towels need replenishing, the plants want water. These may all be helpful things to do, but they can keep a person from the job at hand. Sometimes it seems that the more important a task is the more an ADDer will put it off, finding those perennial "other things" to do.

Remember that ADDers have trouble weighing the importance of tasks—or "sequencing," as some psychologists call it. Watering the plants can have just as much importance as finishing the annual report, at least in the ADDer's mind.

Because the ADDer has a head full of things to do, he or she can begin to feel overwhelmed. How do you cope with being overwhelmed? You knock something off the list. Sometimes this happens naturally as a task is simply forgotten. But sometimes the best strategy to get a task done is to cross it off the list. Which task do you cross off? The one that's easiest to do. So you water the plants, because that will only take a minute, rather than working on that report, which you know will take hours.

The only problem is that those "other" tasks always pop up. While you're getting water for the plants, you notice that the sink needs to be washed. While you're getting the paper towels to wash the sink, you see that you're almost out of towels. When you go to the storage cabinet for towels, you see that it's time to order more paper for the photocopier. You may never get to that report.

This is why organizational experts recommend making lists and sticking to them (but not adding new things to the list). Start out with a few minor tasks, they say, but get those done and then focus on your main work. They also suggest breaking down big tasks into small pieces so you can get the same feeling of accomplishment from doing one page of a report as from sharpening all your pencils.

PROBLEM THREE:
MISSED APPOINTMENTS

One of the results of the ADDer's tendency to be disorganized is chronic lateness or the missing of appointments. In many business settings, this creates huge problems. Employers often assume that the ADDer secretly "wants" to be late or absent, that there is some passive-aggressive rebellion going on. But that is not true at all. The ADDer probably wants to be there on time but honestly forgets or is distracted.

Many missed appointments are simply due to the fact that the ADDer fails to jot down the date and time of the appointment. If the ADDer is not attending to the conversation when the appointment is being made, any arrangements are usually lost. Even when the details are written down, the paper, calendar, or schedule book is often misplaced.

And even when the appointment is remembered, the schedule book is in hand, and the ADDer is heading out the door, there are a million distractions that await. A rosebush may need to be smelled, a car may need to be cleaned, shopping may be necessary, an alternate route may suddenly be tempting—and the person arrives a half-hour late with no idea of where the time went.

PROBLEM FOUR: IMPULSIVE DECISION MAKING

Impulsivity can lead to snap decisions, and snap decisions can hurt a company. In chapter 7, we spoke of the man who bought a house one day—just up and bought it—and then told his wife. He was feeling overwhelmed by all the decisions he had to make and he decided to simplify his life by making a bold move. So he bought a house.

But imagine the employee who buys a company car and then tells his boss. Or the one who decides, on a whim, to change computer systems. Or the secretary who decides to put smiley-faces on all the boss's correspondence.

Decision making is a good thing, especially in business. And there are cases where the impulsivity of an ADDer can come across as a go-getting, take-charge attitude. But a company must also be prepared for those impulsive judgments that are ill-advised. In cases where it would be better to wait a while, to examine the issues, to test various options, to vent an idea with others in the company, the impulsive ADDer is likely to find trouble.

PROBLEM FIVE: RIGID PATTERNS

Because ADDers are so easily distracted, they often develop rigid patterns of action. This seems different from the free-flowing style you might expect from ADDers, but it's a coping mechanism. If they lock into a systematic way of doing things, there are fewer distractions.

The problem is, most businesses operate according to Murphy's Law — if things can go wrong, they will. Modern work situations require flexibility to deal with the various curve balls that are thrown. Some ADDers are brilliant at dreaming up new solutions to challenges, but others are locked into their systems and resist any change.

PROBLEM SIX: THE NEED FOR A COOPERATIVE ENVIRONMENT

What is your workplace like? Visually, is it stark and bare, or are there posters and calendars up on the walls? What does it sound like? Are there voices gabbing, machines humming, music playing softly in the background or blaring at full strength?

ADDers are greatly affected by their environment. Some cannot tolerate any extraneous noise or movement. If there are people rushing past an ADDer's desk, the ADDer may stop to watch. If there is loud music, the ADDer may be drawn away by it.

But the environmental needs are different for

every ADDer. One needs absolute quiet, another gets more distracted by quiet—his mind keeps imagining what's going on "out there." Some need the comfort of masking noise, anything from canned music to tapes of waves crashing on a rocky beach. Others need the stimulation of bright colors and passersby.

The work environment is an important consideration in any company, but it's especially important for ADDers. If they can get everyone to cooperate in creating the environment they need, they can be effective. But in a busy company, such cooperation can be impossible, and the ADD employee will need to work much harder at managing his or her environment.

PROBLEM SEVEN: FAILURE MENTALITY

Some ADDers have had such struggles in life that they assume things will continue to go wrong for them. Their lives have brimmed with great dreams, but again and again they have fallen short of these dreams. Soon they develop a failure mentality; they assume they will not succeed in any new venture.

This can make an ADDer avoid learning situations on the job. While other employees might jump at the chance to take on new responsibilities, the failure-minded ADDer is likely to prefer the same old easy tasks. (This also contributes to rigid patterns, as these ADDers avoid new ways of doing things.)

Imagine the unemployed person who goes out every day looking for work, only to be rejected. After a while, he or she may give up and stay home. "What's the use?" Some ADDers are in exactly that situation, unemployed and giving up. Others are hanging on to low-level jobs, with dashed hopes of advancement.

This is the depressive side of ADD, and the reason many ADDers are originally diagnosed with depression. They have been so buffeted by a cruel world, a world that always seems a step ahead of them, that they lose their will to succeed.

PROBLEM EIGHT:
FRUSTRATION AND ANGER

Maria tells of times when she would get angry with coworkers, or even her boss, and tell them off in no uncertain terms. Now she has learned to anticipate those problems, and she walks away or takes medication or runs six miles.

The ADDer is, in many cases, a simmering pot. All of the frustrations of shattered dreams, missed assignments, and failed attempts have been thrown into that pot, and often it boils over.

This is, of course, the flip side of depression. Some ADDers turn the frustration inward and give up hope. Others turn it outward and rage against everyone in their path.

The littlest thing can set them off. They are angry at people who don't understand them, they are angry at the distractions that keep them from working, they are angry at bosses with unreasonable expectations, they are angry at "the system," they are angry at themselves, they are angry at God, and most of all they are angry at this pain in the neck called Attention Deficit Disorder.

Anger is a natural response to a perceived injustice—and there is plenty of injustice perceived by ADDers. They work so hard, and yet it seems they accomplish little. They deserve better.

239

PROBLEM NINE: IGNORANCE
OF OFFICE POLITICS

Life is political. Not necessarily in a deceitful, underhanded sense, but in the sense of being aware of office politics. This involves knowing what others want to hear and saying it, recognizing who's in power and granting due respect, and getting the right messages across to the right people at the right time.

All of that takes perception and intuition, an ability to read the subtext of conversations and recognize the cues of body language and seemingly off-hand remarks.

Most ADDers don't do that sort of thing. They regularly miss pieces of conversation. They may be extremely perceptive about the pieces they do get, but they're busy trying to reassemble the *text* of the conversation. They don't have time for subtext.

As a result, ADDers may blurt out inappropriate comments. They may violate unwritten rules. They may offend people without knowing it. They're not being rude, they've just missed out on some of the information that everyone else seems to know.

Offices have politics. So do factories and schools and just about any other workplace. There are unwritten rules everywhere, nuances that people are supposed to "get." But ADDers can miss out on this whole underworld of information. As a result, it may seem that they don't fit in.

PROBLEM TEN: HYPERACTIVITY

Maria had trouble sitting still for more than ten minutes. If she were in a meeting with her bosses,

240

she would have to get up and walk around after a while. They may have thought that inappropriate, but she had to do it. It was her hyperactivity. If she didn't move, she would burst.

Most office work is based on a simple physical model: People sit at desks and work. But this is unbearable for hyperactive ADDers. They can sit at desks and work for, say, ten minutes, but then they have to stretch their legs. This is one reason why several of the people we have counseled for ADD have gone into sales — they have left the confinement of the office to go out on the road where they can move more freely.

But *mental* hyperactivity is also an issue for ADDers on the job. In meetings their minds often proceed at a quicker pace than the minds of their coworkers. If an ADDer is running a meeting, he or she may move quickly from point to point without reaching closure on any of the points. The meeting results in much discussed but nothing decided. Other participants in these meetings feel worn out afterward. In a way, they've been introduced to the ADD experience — many ideas being juggled at the same time.

Even as participants in meetings, ADDers can come up with brilliant ideas but say them at the wrong times. Alert bosses will jot down these ideas and reintroduce them at the proper time, but many great ideas get lost because no one else was on the same page.

In some cases, hyperactive ADDers are social butterflies. Many ADDers are good with people. Their energy makes them fun to be with, and they have fun talking with others. In an office or other workplace, these people can be good for morale. They can also cut down on office productivity, not

241

only their own, but also that of the people they talk with.

Again, most of these "social butterflies" don't intend to cheat their companies out of man-hours, but they find a certain amount of success in their social contacts that often eludes them in their desk work. Every time a person walks by, these ADDers are drawn toward a "successful" conversation they might have with that person.

This is another reason why many ADDers thrive in jobs that allow them a great deal of contact with people, such as sales. They use the positive aspects of their love of socializing, rather than fighting the negative aspects of desk work.

How to Succeed in the Workplace

Seek treatment. We know we're sounding like a broken record, but many of the problems cited above can be lessened with a proper course of ADD treatment, including medication, counseling, and behavior modification.

Communicate your needs to boss and coworkers. Some people try to hide their ADD, but there's no need for that. People around you probably know there's *something* amiss. If they know *what* it is, chances are that their response would improve.

It's best not to make demands in the workplace — insisting that they change the environment or ways of doing business just to suit you. But if you present the idea that you want to be a productive worker, and certain changes will increase your productivity for the company, you may get the accommodations without much fuss.

Although we feel that the Americans with Disabilities Act is sometimes abused, it does serve to

242

create a climate in which companies are more apt to make reasonable accommodations than to fire you. If you communicate your needs properly, you may succeed in getting some changes made.

Find your place. There are aspects of ADD—creativity, broad thinking, energy—that can make you a very good worker. Other aspects, as we have seen, can create problems. You need to find a job that uses your strengths and minimizes your weaknesses.

This may mean leaving your company and finding a job elsewhere. Or perhaps you can work with the personnel office in your present company to find another niche for you there. Or maybe you can talk with your boss and arrange different responsibilities for you.

Set reasonable expectations. Much of the frustration related to ADD is a combination of lofty dreams and limited realities. You can see where you want to go—you can see that probably better than most people—but you can't seem to get there.

As you take steps to increase your productivity, you could also take steps to make your dreams more realistic. Get a sense of what you can reasonably accomplish today, this week, this month. Don't set impossible deadlines or standards you will never reach. It might help to work with someone else in setting your *reasonable* goals.

Develop a system of small tasks and immediate rewards. What's the main project you have to do at work right now? How long do you think it will take you to finish? How much of it do you think you can do today? How much can you do in the next hour? What about the next half hour?

Big tasks intimidate the ADDer. That's why so many waste time on trivial little tasks. What's the answer? Making your big task into a series of small tasks. You can decide how small the segments need to be, depending on your usual attention span. But it would not be unreasonable to work on a report a page at a time, or some other assignment a half hour at a time.

When you finish the mini-task, reward yourself in a small way. Get up and take a brief walk. Eat something. Make a phone call. Talk for two minutes with a coworker. Or even water the plants.

Don't let the reward get out of hand, though. Limit the time of the reward to about 10 percent of the time worked. Then plunge back into the next small portion of your main task.

Get the right people around you. If you are a manager or boss, you should be able to hire people whose abilities complement yours. If you aren't, you may still be able to team up with certain employees by letting your boss know who you work well with.

You need people who are organized and patient. In some cases, these people have limited vision. They don't look at the big picture. That's what you bring to the team. By finding others with complementary skills, you create a synergy that helps everyone work better.

Arrange your work space as best you can. If you have control over where your desk is, what's on the walls, what music is playing, and so on, make the choices that help you work best.

Do you need no distraction, mild (masking) background, or lots of stimulation? You may need to experiment with different arrangements before you find the best one. Ask others to help you with your "testing" of various options. (Sometimes people think they know the best conditions to work under, but they're mistaken. Test it out.)

Try a buddy system. If you are fortunate enough to have a close friend as a coworker, rely on that friend to fill in some of the gaps for you. You may blurt out inappropriate things without knowing it. You may not hear certain details of an important assignment. You may be spending too much time away from your work station, talking with others. A good friend can help you in all these cases.

Don't be shy about asking for help. Give your friend permission to tell you what you need to hear — even if it's unpleasant. Ask for permission to ask "dumb" questions if you think you missed something. Maybe you could even get regular "How am I doing?" checkups. Be accountable to that person for your behavior on the job.

Working with a Person Who Has ADD

IF YOU'RE THE BOSS . . .

An ADDer may photocopy pages 245-248 for his or her boss. Limited permission is granted for this purpose.

Working with an ADDer can be an exhilarating experience. It can also try your patience. What "reasonable accommodations" can you make in order to bring out the best of what an employee with Attention Deficit Disorder has to offer? As we have said repeatedly, ADDers tend to be quite creative. Many have a breadth to their thinking that spawns new ideas. That is, they may be in a discussion of marketing strategies, but they're thinking about production and personnel and future planning at the same time. This kind of thinking can create breakthroughs for a company.

245

But in the daily grind of crunching numbers, filling out forms, and writing reports, they may fall short of expectations. It is not a lack of desire or of intelligence, but a physical difference in the brain that causes *inconsistency* of attention.

This situation demands understanding and creative solutions. How do you use the pluses of the ADDer while minimizing the minuses? Here are some possibilities.

Rearrange the work space. Talk with the ADDer about the conditions that are best for his or her productivity. Some respond well to busy-ness and noise, others are overly distracted. We understand that a whole office can't be overhauled for one employee, but reasonable accommodations should be considered. Perhaps a private office with a door could do the trick, or a change in the background music. Discuss the various options with the ADDer and the whole staff.

Hire complementary personnel. A manager with ADD can suggest bold new directions for the business, but will probably not follow through. Can you hire secretaries, assistants, and other managers who will follow through? The ADDer in your office is probably a visionary. You need a detail person to fill the gaps.

Hold structured meetings. The ADDer has trouble structuring his or her own thinking, so it helps when meetings or other communication have structure to them. That is, prepare a written agenda. Number the points. That way, if the ADDer blinks for a minute, he or she will know what was missed.

Repeat and review. It helps if you ask an ADDer to summarize the content of a meeting or the details of an assignment. That way, you'll know if the information got through. If you develop a nonjudgmental spirit with the ADDer, he or she will not try to fake it but will acknowledge parts of the meeting or discussion that were missed. At the end of an important presentation, repeat the main points.

You might also allow the ADDer to tape meetings so the information can be reviewed on his or her own time.

Put things in writing. Write down assignments in detail. It might help to have a note-taker at important meetings who will distribute the notes to those present, including the person with ADD. It is practically impossible for many ADDers to take good notes, since they have to split their attention between listening and writing.

Set intermediate deadlines. If you leave ADDers on their own for projects that take six months, they (and you) may be in trouble. Set monthly or bi-weekly deadlines on an extended project so the ADDer is accountable on a regular basis.

Find the right responsibilities for the ADDer. There are some tasks that ADDers have great difficulty with — generally detail-oriented "busy-work." Of course, many people have difficulty with that, but for many ADDers such work is basically impossible. They become distracted by anything and everything. On the other hand, work with creative ideas, work with people, and physically active work can be areas of success for ADDers.

Allow for "exercise breaks." Not all ADDers are hyperactive, but many are. If you have a hyperactive ADDer in your office, you'll know it. It's the person who seems to be walking around the desk more than sitting at it. They pace during meetings or have to leave the room. Or they're always fidgeting.

Hyperactive ADDers just *have to* move around. It will benefit the company if you encourage regular movement breaks.

Certainly you may come up with other ways to make the best use of your ADD employees, recognizing their distinctive challenges. Creativity, flexibility, and patience are crucial.

IF YOU'RE A COWORKER . . . .

An ADDer may photocopy pages 248-249 for his or her coworkers. Limited permission is given for this purpose.

Working alongside a person with ADD can be a challenge, though it also has its rewards. Many of the "reasonable accommodations" listed above can be adapted to one-on-one situations. Note especially the point on "Repeat and Review." You may need to go over information a second or third time before the ADDer gets it.

Expect and accept some frustration and anger. ADDers have to contend with a lot. They usually have big dreams and bigger limitations. They have piled up years of frustration with their own underachievement. That frustration may spill over onto you. In most cases, they're not really mad at you. They're mad at themselves or at their ADD. Try to understand their anger and let it roll off you.

Be a buddy. People with ADD need people without ADD to help them. They need to be able to ask questions about things that you've both just heard or seen. They need people to tell them when they've forgotten something important or said something out of line. You can be that person.

Be considerate, but don't be dominated.
You need patience in working with an ADDer. It can be tiring to repeat things, follow through, and make up for the gaps in the ADDer's memory. Sometimes, however, your "patience" can contribute to a sort of codependent relationship.

You need to establish boundaries of just what you will and will not do for the person with ADD. When you start to feel used, talk about it and develop new ways of doing things. The ADDer needs to be accountable for his or her own behavior. We hope you can develop a give-and-take arrangement with the ADDer where there is mutual benefit.

Affirm the positive characteristics of the person with ADD. Sometimes it seems that the ADDer is intentionally slacking off, not trying to listen, or intentionally being rude. But this is seldom the case. Their brains are not firing exactly right, and occasionally they lose the ability to say no to distraction. In most cases they *are* trying, harder than you know. And in most cases, they deserve applause and respect for coping with their difficulties as well as they have.

ADDers are often energetic and enjoyable. They are often brilliantly creative. Whenever you can, affirm the person for these (and other) positive qualities. Because of the problems they have faced, many ADDers have poor self-esteem. They regularly give themselves "You're no good" messages. You can help to counteract those messages by offering sincere praise.

JUST THE FACTS

- The workplace may present many difficulties for the adult with ADD, as well as for those who work with him or her. The ADDer faces at least ten problem areas at work, including the tendency to "blink" at important moments, to become easily distracted, to start projects but not finish them, and to struggle with personal attitudes and relationships with coworkers.

- Effective solutions to these problems are discussed at length on pages 242-245 ("How to Succeed in the Workplace"). They include communicating your needs to your colleagues and making your relationships work for you, working out of your strengths and setting reasonable expectations, breaking down tasks into small pieces, improving your work space, and seeking effective ADD treatment.

- If you work with someone whose ADD appears untreated, you may be highly frustrated! Pages 245-249 offer suggestions on how to cope as well as how to help.

Advice from the Trenches: A Conclusion

We have shared the stories of many people with ADD, stories with different details and different outcomes. You have met some people who are being treated for ADD and some who remain untreated. You have seen the struggles, the failed relationships, the lost jobs, and unrealized dreams. But you have also read about people who have succeeded in overcoming the most crippling aspects of their ADD and are enjoying effective, fulfilling lives.

> "Attitude is a little thing that makes a big difference."

We believe the greatest difference in outcome is due not to the severity of the symptoms but to the attitude of the person with ADD.

What does the diagnosis of ADD mean to you? It's not a death sentence, not even close. ADDers can live wonderfully exciting and productive lives. We have seen the life-changing effect of the proper diagnosis and treatment of ADD in the lives of those with the disorder and in the lives of their families, friends, and colleagues.

251

ADD is not an excuse, a way to duck responsibility. It is a challenge that can be met and overcome. Those who meet the challenge of ADD, rather than rolling over and playing dead, are the ones who succeed.

We asked several people with ADD what they would say to someone who isn't sure but thinks he or she might have ADD. Here's their advice:

- There is no harm in checking it out.
- If you think you might have it, pursue it and find out. Not knowing is worse than knowing.
- It helped me to know there was a reason for my problems. By taking medication I can now learn anything!
- Knowing about ADD has hugely affected my self-esteem. There is so much mourning that goes with ADD. Find out about it and get on with your life.
- It is a disability of sorts, but there is an answer. People should realize it is not merely a matter of attitude or exercise. You have to have help to overcome it.
- Change the acronym for ADD to Accept . . . Do . . . Dream.[1]

ACCEPT

The first step in attitude adjustment is to accept the way we are made: some with ADD; some without; and others with some of the symptoms.

Accepting means having your eyes wide open and having accurate information about yourself. You may need to accept that you have ADD and learn to face the future with this new knowledge.

252

Acceptance means you are not angry about it, you don't blame others for your problem, and you take full responsibility for your treatment.

On the other hand, you might have to accept that you *don't* have ADD. Facing the truth might involve the realization that you have ADD-type symptoms, but that these are due to some other condition such as depression, anxiety, or an overactive thyroid. In either case, it is your responsibility to get the proper treatment.

> "Accept the challenges of your life so that you may feel the exhilaration of success."

DO

After you have accepted your diagnosis, do something about it. That usually means seeking treatment! Schedule that appointment you've been putting off, pursue a trial medication, or begin planning the reorganization of your life. You may not want to spend the time or money necessary to make such changes, but these investments are potentially life-changing, not only for you but also for those you love. How else will you know what you might accomplish by taking those first few steps toward change?

> "You become successful the moment you start moving toward a worthwhile goal."

When you do something, however, make sure you avoid the impulsive style of the past. Changing jobs, starting a new business, or making a major move is not the kind of decision you want to make without sound advice and caution. Instead, doing something about your condition might mean building into your life a level of accountability that will help you to avoid impulsive, regrettable decisions.

DREAM

Now dream your dreams! Once you understand your condition and have taken steps to treat it, there is no reason you can't reach for your dreams. In fact, many ADDers have been quite successful in their endeavors.

What about you? What are your dreams? The only way to start turning your dreams into realities is to take that first step.

> "If one advances confidently in the direction of their dreams, and endeavors to lead a life which they have imagined, they will meet with a success unexpected in common hours."
>
> —*Henry David Thoreau*

NOTE

1. This idea came from Maria Bassler, whose story we told in chapter 8.

AUTHORS

THOMAS A. WHITEMAN, PH.D., has dealt extensively with childhood ADD and is now a psychologist in private practice specializing in diagnosing and treating adults with ADD. He is the founder and president of Life Counseling Services, a counseling center that employs sixteen therapists, three psychologists, and two psychiatrists, all under Dr. Whiteman's direction. He is also the president of Fresh Start Seminars, a nonprofit organization that conducts over fifty divorce recovery seminars a year throughout the United States for both adults and children. Dr. Whiteman is the author of eight books.

MICHELE NOVOTNI, PH.D., is a psychologist in private practice at Life Counseling Services and a certified school psychologist. Dr. Novotni is also a professor at Eastern College in a graduate level counseling program and is a clinical supervisor in the student counseling center where she developed a diagnostic and treatment program for college students with ADD. Dr. Novotni is a frequent speaker on the topic of adult ADD and has extensive experience in the areas of child and adult ADD, learning disabilities, and behavior management. Both her son and her father have ADD.

INDEX

Relaxation, 116
Remembering, failure to, 55
Residual ADD, 60. *See also*
    Attention Deficit Disor-
    der (ADD)
Resnick, Robert, 53
Response inhibition, 102
Response management, 102
Responsibility
    of ADDer, 35-36, 38-41,
    43, 227, 253
    coping skills and, 21
    of family, to find treatment,
    36
    of schools, and ADDers,
    35-36
Rigid patterns, at workplace,
    231, 237, 238
Risk taking, 25, 215
Ritalin, 51, 63, 111, 144, 165

Sadness. *See* Depression
Schachar and Tannock, 101
Schizophrenia, 53
School. *See also* Learning
    accommodation for
    ADDers and, 30, 35-
    36, 209, 210
    problems for ADDers in,
    39, 120
Screening, 25, 62. *See also*
    Assessment
    by master level counselor,
    74, 77, 78
    Novotni ADD Screening
    Assessment, 67-69
    of self, 67-69. *See also*
    Self-diagnosis
    by social worker, 75, 78,
    83
Seizure disorders, 92
"Selective forgetting," 200
Selective Serotonin-Reuptake
    Inhibitors (SSRIs), 143,
    144-145
Self-centeredness, 33
Self-confidence, 170

Self-diagnosis, 62
    danger of, 50, 53, 58
Self-doubt, 22
Self-esteem
    building of, 142-143, 159,
    208
    effects of ADD on, 155,
    157, 163, 252
    hyperactivity and, 110
    poor, 195, 203, 228, 249.
    See also Self-image,
    low
Self-focus, 218-220, 230
Self-image, low, 22, 24, 33,
    168, 220-222, 230. *See
    also* Self-esteem, poor
Self-organization, 183-189,
    195-196. *See also*
    Organization
Self-reporting, 88-89, 95, 151
Self-screening. *See* Screening,
    of self
Self-talk, 202-203, 208
Serotonin, 144
Shame, 10
Side effect, of medication,
    144, 149, 153
"Signposts," to improve atten-
    tion, 132
Silver, Larry, 91, 207
Simidion, Mark, 37-38
Sitting, difficulty of, 54, 113
Skills, academic, 156, 163
Skills, social, 156-157, 163
Social nuances, 25, 39, 156,
    211
Social workers, in ADD treat-
    ment, 75, 78
Space management, 189-191,
    196, 244-246, 250. *See
    also* Stuff management
Spelling, problems with, 47
SSRIs (Selective Serotonin-
    Reuptake Inhibitors),
    143, 144-145